A Place of Beauty

A Place of Beauty

The Artists and Gardens of the Cornish Colony

Alma M. Gilbert & Judith B. Tankard

TEN SPEED PRESS
Berkeley Toronto

(page i) The view from Charles A. Platt's studio to the Cornish hills, circa 1903. Courtesy of members of the Platt family.

(previous page) An early view of Stephen Parrish's garden, with Anne and Lydia (in window) Parrish, 1898. Photo by Stephen Parrish. Alma Gilbert Collection.

(below) Anne Parrish in the balcony at Northcote, 1898. Photo by Maxfield Parrish. Alma Gilbert Collection.

TEN SPEED PRESS
PO Box 7123
Berkeley, California 94707
www.tenspeed.com

Distributed in Australia by Simon and Schuster Australia, in Canada by Ten Speed Press Canada, in New Zealand by Southern Publishers Group, in South Africa by Real Books, in Southeast Asia by Berkeley Books, and in the United Kingdom and Europe by Airlift Books.

Cover and Text Design by Jeff Puda

Library of Congress Cataloging-in-Publication Data on file with publisher.

First printing, 2000
Printed in Hong Kong

1 2 3 4 5 6 7 8 9 10—03 02 01 00

Contents

Art, Beauty and the Landscapes of the Cornish Colony

Alma M. Gilbert

The Gardens of the Cornish Colony

Judith B. Tankard

Acknowledgments

A complicated book such as *A Place of Beauty* could not have come into being without the help and cooperation of a number of individuals, historical societies, galleries, and museums. The authors would like to acknowledge the following: Philip N. Cronenwett, Curator of Manuscripts, and his staff at Special Collections, Dartmouth College Library, Hanover, N.H.; Henry Duffy and Gregory C. Schwarz, Saint-Gaudens National Historic Site, Cornish, N.H.; Cornish Colony Gallery and Museum, Cornish, N.H.; Wanda Styka, Chesterwood National Trust for Historic Preservation, Stockbridge, Mass.; Rare and Manuscripts Collection, Cornell University, Ithaca, N.Y.; Detroit Institute of Art, Detroit, Mich.; National Museum of Art, Smithsonian Institution, Washington, D.C.; Lorna Condon, Society for the Preservation of New England Antiquities, Boston; Meg Nowack, Woodrow Wilson House, Washington, D.C.; James B. Atkinson, Cornish Historical Society, Cornish, N.H.; Plainfield Historical Society, Plainfield, N.H.; Beacon Hill Fine Arts, New York; Berry-Hill Galleries, New York; Comenos Fine Arts, Boston; Hirschl and Adler Galleries, New York; Spanierman Gallery, New York; Louise Todd Ambler; Max Blumberg and Eduardo Araujo; Lois Bromley; Grace Bulkeley; Shirley DeWald; Robert Gordon and Marjorie Mann; Karen and Doug Heaton; May Brawley Hill; the Henry Hyde family; Marilyn Gage Hyson; Ann and Tony Neidecker; Bill Noble; Peter S. Nyboer; William Pear; Ron Pisano; Charles and Joan Platt; the Prellwitz family; George Reed and Yvonne Mathieu; Dean Rouston; Charles Shurcliff; Nancy Angell Streeter; Anne Tracy; Margery P. Trumbull; the Henry Walker family; John and Connie White; and many others.

And David Putnam of Claremont, N.H., for his beautiful photography of the gardens.

ALMA M. GILBERT
JUDITH B. TANKARD

Introduction

A thing of beauty is a joy forever:
Its loveliness increases; it will never
Pass into nothingness; but still will keep
A bower quiet for us, and a sleep
Full of sweet dreams, and health, and quiet breathing.
—*John Keats*

*I*n the early years of the twentieth century, the artists' colony in Cornish, New Hampshire, was considered one of the most beautifully gardened villages in America. "Cornish is a charming spot, a mecca for artists and cultivated people. The chief rivalry among these delightful folk seemed to be who could make the loveliest garden. . . . there seems to be about it all a halo of gorgeous color from the flowers," reminisced Edith Bolling Galt (the second Mrs. Woodrow Wilson) about her visit to the colony in 1915.[1] That tradition is still a treasured part of the Cornish area today, where gardens old and new flourish.

When the popular press discovered the rural art colony in the early 1900s, it was singled out for its "alluring charm," "unconscious simplicity," and other "seductive factors."[2] One of those factors was its inimitable artists' gardens. That these gardens were designed, created, and maintained by artists made them all the more appealing. Rose Standish Nichols, one of the colony's resident garden writers and an accomplished gardener herself, explained the magic of Cornish gardens: "Charming gardens were created by struggling artists who hardly knew the commonest flowers by name, but who were thoroughly conversant with the principles of design. Every householder was his own head gardener and landscape architect, though subject to much constructive criticism from his neighbors."[3]

Not only were the colony's gardens outstanding, but the area boasted a cluster of houses designed to magically blend with the natural landscape. They ranged from modest farmhouses fixed up by their discerning homeowners to architectural gems designed by Charles Platt, Wilson Eyre, and other names in the emerging world of American country house architecture. Gardens conceived as outdoor living spaces were part and parcel with these houses, where entertaining and enjoyment of the magnificent scenery were a main sustenance. The colony's preponderance of architect-designed houses with intimate garden "rooms" parallels the Arts and Crafts movement in Britain before World War I. This era saw the building of small houses and gardens inspired by William Morris, C. F. A. Voysey, M. H. Baillie Scott, and other designers and architects who revered fine craftsmanship and vernacular sensibilities. Illustrations of these small-scaled homes and gardens that appeared in periodicals and books inspired many American architects and designers.

"Cornish" is somewhat of a misnomer, since the colony was spread out over Windsor, Vermont, as well as the villages of Plainfield and Cornish in New Hampshire. Herbert Adams, Winston Churchill, William Hart, Maxfield Parrish, and the Shipmans all lived in Plainfield. Ellen Shipman ensured her attachment to the colony in her playful calling cards— "Geographically in Plainfield, Socially in Cornish." Cornish, with its loose geographic boundaries, was more a state of mind.

And yet, the colony's unique character was undeniably linked to its sense of place: a place of beauty. The region's highly acclaimed natural beauty was undoubtedly what attracted its many artists. The idyllic scenery, with rolling hills resembling an Italian landscape and fairytale views across the Connecticut River Valley to Mount Ascutney in Vermont, provided a magically stimulating atmosphere for the creation of art.

The creative journey begins in the artist's mind and heart. Inspired by beauty and fueled by the love, passion, or exaltation that beauty awakens, the artist discovers a yearning to re-create that which has touched or moved him. In this way, the perception of beauty has engendered many a work of art, whether painting, sculpture, photography, or the special palette of gardens created by those who revere the glories of nature.

In Cornish there briefly converged this enchanting combination: A place of beauty, its passionate appreciation, and the consequent desire to create, in turn, equally inspiring objects and places of beauty. The fruits of that creative drive are what we reap today: The countless paintings, sculptures, writings, and of course, gardens live on, planting seeds of inspiration that are still being harvested.

Perhaps, in a way, the artists at Cornish sought to re-create Cornish itself, or at least the sublime feeling the place inspired. As Ellen Shipman's calling card attested, after all, Cornish was to its residents not so much a place, as a state of mind.

ALMA M. GILBERT
JUDITH B. TANKARD

Maxfield Parrish, *Janion's Maple*, oil on board, 1956. Private Collection.

These are the things I prize
And hold of dearest worth:
Light of the sapphire skies,
Peace of the silent hills,
Shelter of the forests, comfort of the grass,
Music of birds, murmur of little rills,
Shadows of clouds that swiftly pass,
And after showers,
The smell of flowers
And of the good brown earth
And best of all, along the way, friendship and mirth.

Henry Van Dyke

I

Art, Beauty and the Landscapes of the Cornish Colony

by Alma M. Gilbert

(above) The vine-covered loggia at The Oaks, circa 1910. Alma Gilbert Collection.

(bottom) Maxfield Parrish in a contemplative mood enjoying his garden from his porch, circa 1920. Dartmouth College Library.

CHAPTER 1

A Brief History of the Cornish Colony

Some of Cornish's earliest settlers were Bryants and Chases, who sailed up the Connecticut River in the mid-1700s. Their descendants included Salmon Portland Chase, secretary of the treasury and chief justice of the United States under President Lincoln. Another descendant of those early settlers, Captain Chester Pike (1829–1897), had one of the largest farms in New Hampshire with over a thousand acres of rolling pastures, spectacular vistas spilling from Mount Ascutney—the dormant volcano that overlooks the town from neighboring Vermont—down to the Connecticut River.

During one of Salmon Portland Chase's visits to his homestead in Cornish, he visited Chester Pike and introduced him to Charles C. Beaman, an up-and-coming young New York lawyer in the law firm of William Maxwell Evarts. Evarts had served President Lincoln well during the Civil War as legal adviser overseas and in 1881 had been named secretary of state by President Rutherford B. Hayes. Evarts owned vast amounts of land across the Connecticut River in Windsor, Vermont. His home, Juniper Hill, was dubbed by many as President Hayes's Summer White House. Beaman had just married Evarts's daughter, Hettie Sherman Evarts. Both her parents and her new husband wanted the young marrieds to settle near the Evarts family home, where they would be surrounded by lush rolling hills with fantastic views of the mountains, the woods, and the river. Juniper Hill, shining white across

(left) Saint-Gaudens family on porch, circa 1898. Dartmouth College Library.

(top) Postcard view of the steep road up to Dingleton Hill, 1920s. Courtesy of Grace Bulkeley.

the river, was visible from Pike's land, an easy buggy ride across a covered bridge into Vermont. Chester Pike's land was the logical spot for the newlyweds. Beaman purchased several hundred acres of Pike's land, and soon settled into the area with his new wife.

Wishing to increase the local social life of the area, Beaman began an aggressive plan to "colonize" the area by purchasing local farms and homes and renting or selling them to his friends—established artists, writers, and politicians—to form what he called a "Little New York." Much to the astonishment of the local farmers, these interlopers began not only buying up the old farms, but transforming them into summer homes replete with large studios and ornamental gardens that went well beyond vegetable plots. His first tenant was the famous sculptor Augustus Saint-Gaudens, who helped form what became known as the Cornish Art Colony. In 1885, Beaman lured the famed sculptor (among whose sitters were such famous personages as Mrs. Grover Cleveland, John Singer

(opposite) Mrs. Grover Cleveland modeling for Saint-Gaudens, 1887. Photo by Richard Watson Gilder. Dartmouth College Library.

(left) Thomas Wilmer Dewing, circa 1880–90. Freer Gallery of Art Archives, Smithsonian Institution, Washington, D.C.

(below) Maria Richards Oakey (Dewing), 1872. Hobbs, *The Art of Thomas Wilmer Dewing*, 1996.

Sargent, and Robert Louis Stevenson) by promising him plenty of "Lincoln-shaped men" when the artist was immersed in working on Chicago's famed standing *Lincoln* statue (1884-1887).

After renting for a year or so to see whether Cornish suited him, Saint-Gaudens and his wife, Augusta, purchased land and a house—a former tavern (and some say former house of ill repute)—from Beaman. He renamed their home Aspet for a town in France where his family had once lived. Saint-Gaudens's presence was the catalyst that brought other artists and friends to the area. Shortly after Saint-Gaudens settled in Cornish, Dr. Arthur Nichols, a prominent Boston physician married to Elizabeth Homer, Augusta Saint-Gaudens's sister, bought the remaining Chester Pike property and settled in historic Mastlands, named after the tall pines that had supplied masts for purveyors of the King's navy. Along with his wife, Dr. Nichols brought his three daughters: Rose (Saint-Gaudens's favorite), Marian, and Margaret, the youngest, a firebrand.

The first artists who moved into the area after Saint-Gaudens were Thomas and Maria Dewing (1886), George de Forest Brush (1887), Henry and Laura Walker (1888), and Stephen Parrish (1893).

Stephen's son, Maxfield Parrish, perhaps the best remembered of all the Cornish Colony artists, followed his father to New Hampshire in 1898.

Having met Saint-Gaudens and his friend, architect Charles Platt, while studying in Paris, Henry Walker commissioned Charles Platt to design the first of many homes in Cornish. In 1890, after renting locally for two summers, the Walkers moved into their new summer home replete with vistas, whispering pines, a rushing mountain brook, and cascading water that later served as the local swimming pool for other members of the colony. Platt built his own house close to his friends the Walkers in 1891. Later that same year, Daniel Chester French, another well-known sculptor of the day—renowned for his statue of Concord's *Minute Man* and two of the nation's capital's most famous memorials, the seated *Lincoln* and *Victory: The First Division's War Memorial*—rented a home located on what is now known as Platt Road.

Daniel and Mary French spent three summers in Cornish living at what is now called Barberry House while he worked on the gigantic sixty-five-foot-high statue of *The Republic* for the World's Columbian Exposition in Chicago. A friend and

(above) Stephen and Anne Parrish at the beach, circa 1920. Dartmouth College Library.

(right) Mabel Harlakenden (Mrs. Winston Churchill), circa 1895. Child, *History of the Town of Cornish New Hampshire*, 1910.

(far right) Winston Churchill, circa 1898. Dartmouth College Library.

contemporary of Saint-Gaudens, French often good-naturedly teased the slightly older sculptor with mock competitiveness. Before Saint-Gaudens invited French to use his studio while he worked on *The Republic*, French wrote Saint-Gaudens from Paris in July 1887:

> *I have been enjoying immensely my sojourn in Paris and wish I might stay another winter. I shall however return home next month—I hope a littler wiser than I came, so look to your laurels!*[1]

In her book *Memories*, Laura Walker writes of the natural kindness, courtesy, and gentle spirits exhibited by both her neighbors Saint-Gaudens and French. She describes some of the charades and dinners held by local artists, including Stephen and Maxfield Parrish. Two other popular members of the group were American writer Winston

Churchill and Mabel Harlakenden, his attractive wife who posed frequently for Maxfield Parrish. Annie Lazarus, whose sister Emma was the poet who wrote the famous inscription on the Statue of Liberty, "Give me your tired, your poor…," also moved to Cornish in the 1890s. Charles Platt designed and built homes for Annie Lazarus, Winston Churchill, and Augusta and Emily Slade.

The colony lured many other artists, including Herbert Adams and his beautiful wife Adeline Pond Adams (a biographer of some note), Kenyon Cox, Henry and Lucia Fuller, Ethel Barrymore, Henry and Edith Prellwitz, Frederic Remington, and William Henry Hyde.

Writers and publishers joined the exodus to Cornish, including such famous names as Herbert Croly, founding editor of the *New Republic*; editor and playwright Louis Evan Shipman, whose wife Ellen Shipman became an accomplished landscape

(left) Charles A. Platt, circa 1920. Photo by Pirie MacDonald. Courtesy of the members of the Platt family.

(below) Daniel Chester French, *Mary and Margaret French*, pastel, 1893. Chesterwood, Stockbridge, Massachusetts.

architect under the tutelage of Charles Platt; Norman Hapgood, editor of *Collier's*; Maxwell Evarts Perkins, the powerful editor of *Scribner's* (his wife, Louise Saunders, wrote the famous Parrish illustrated children's book *Knave of Hearts*); and poet Percy MacKaye.

Musicians such as composer Arthur Whiting; singer and pianist Grace Lawrence and her sister Edith; the Fuller sisters, Cynthia, Dorothy, and Rosalind; opera singer Louise Homer; and even dancer Isadora Duncan moved to the colony and entertained members at soirees at Maxfield Parrish's house, The Oaks; the Nichols ballroom at Mastlands; Churchill's Harlakenden; the terraced garden of the Slade sisters' Dingleton House; or the music room at Annie Lazarus's High Court.

Soon, yet another wave of visitors arrived. Politicians such as Presidents Teddy Roosevelt and Woodrow Wilson visited and summered in the area. Mr. Wilson rented Harlakenden, Winston Churchill's palatial home from 1913 to 1915. Judge Learned Hand, whose attractive daughters posed for many of Maxfield Parrish's works, lived near Saint-Gaudens. William Jennings Bryan, whose granddaughter Kitty Owen posed for the Parrish oil *Daybreak*, was also a frequent summer visitor.

Although the natural beauty of Cornish had been the lure for the first of the area's talented residents, the growing concentration of intellectual and creative talent in the region soon became an alluring force of its own. The opportunity for artists and intellectuals to pool energies and gifts in such a stimulating, beautiful environment is what, ultimately, destined Cornish for its rich artistic heritage.

(above) Dinner at High Court, August 1892. Left to right: Edith Prellwitz, Annie Lazarus (with back to camera), Devereux Emmet, Thomas Dewing, Elizabeth Dewing, Maria Oakey Dewing, and Howard Hart. Photo by Henry Prellwitz. Courtesy U.S. Department of the Interior, National Park Service, Saint-Gaudens National Historic Site, Cornish, N.H.

(opposite) Laura Walker and her son Marq watching "four o'clocks" bloom in their garden in Cornish, circa 1892. Photo by Henry Walker. Courtesy of Jacqueline Walker Smith.

CHAPTER 2

Life in the Cornish Colony

Diaries and memoirs written by various colony members share insightful anecdotes, revealing the colony's unique lifestyle. It was well known among both residents and summer visitors, for example, that the artists were very serious about their work time. It was absolutely taboo to visit one of the working artists during "work hours" unless one were consulting about a work in progress. Laura Walker writes in her *Memories*:

> In the earliest days great simplicity reigned and hard work every morning for all those who were of the professions. The wives, unless they too painted or wrote, tended to their household cares, etc. And in the afternoons there was relaxation from work—visiting and tennis and trips and picnics, and whatever.
>
> In the evenings we often had acting—mostly of impromptu nature and by all means very good and a great delight to us. There were certain ones who were apt to be chosen but all could take a hand.[2]

Frances Grimes, a sculptor who worked as an assistant to Saint-Gaudens from 1901 until the time of his death in 1907, refers to Cornish as a state of mind and a "cult of beauty." In *Reminiscences*, she echoes Walker:

> It was the rule that no one ever paid a visit in the morning or before four o'clock in the afternoon. This rule was broken when an artist was invited to see another's work for criticism or consultation, these were weighty visits, visits of state.[3]

(opposite) Maxfield Parrish, tennis enthusiast, circa 1885. Photo by Stephen Parrish. Dartmouth College Library.

(left) Henry and Laura Walker, circa 1888. Courtesy of John and Connie White.

Grimes also mused on Cornish's seemingly extraordinary reserve of beautiful women:

What was seen in the sense, the pictorial sense, was so important! Gowns that were praised there would not have been praised on Fifth Avenue. They were gowns that painters would like to paint. This point of view perhaps explains why so many of the women in Cornish had unusual beauty, for I am sure they had unusual beauty! [4]

The following story illustrates her observation:

One day I returned from a drive saying I had just met the most lovely girl I had ever seen. I had seen her walking at the foot of our hill and did not know who she was. She was tall and slender with golden hair curling back from her face. . . . When I knew her later I could always realize that it was not merely the exquisite drawn nose or the forms around her eyes that made her lovely, but could see in her the distinction of a Tanagra figurine. It was Anne Parrish who had come to live with her cousin Stephen Parrish. [5]

During summer afternoons, the artists visited. Many of the country places had tennis courts; Mastlands, High Court, Harlakenden, Brook Place,

the Platts, the Houstons, and later the Rublees all had clay courts, which their friends and neighbors often enjoyed. Margaret Nichols, who was a tennis and archery enthusiast and one of the earliest female professional tennis players, tells a story in her *Lively Days: Some Memoirs of Margaret Homer Shurcliff:*

Once when I was playing in a tournament against Fred (Maxfield) Parrish, we were being umpired by Kenyon Cox who didn't play, but loved to officiate. I beat Fred roundly and he came around to complain ruefully that our incompetent umpire had given me too many points on form and not given him enough points on style. I laughed and told Mr. Cox to give him a few more points for style, since at four months pregnant my form was nothing to brag on. I still beat him, despite my "handicap." [6]

In 1888, Henry and Laura Walker were asked to house-sit the Saint-Gaudens's Aspet. The house was supposed to come equipped with a cook who had not yet materialized when the couple arrived. Laura details in her *Memories* the following anecdote:

The house was large and had to be well kept. There was washing and ironing and cooking, and guests came and I had my hands too full— so suddenly having it all to do.

Winter sports by the Parrish children:
Dillwyn, Jean, Stephen, and Max Jr. in a
slide built for their enjoyment by their
father, circa 1915. Dartmouth College
Library.

*For instance, one day when I was for the first
time in my life exploring the depths of a chicken,
Henry came rushing in and said, 'You must
come, a party from Walpole in a coach with their
guests—Stanford White and others are here—
What can we give them?'*

*Hurriedly washing my hands, sticking in
a few hairpins, and tearing off my apron, I went
out on the piazza and lemonade and cake were
all we could offer in the way of refreshments, as
well as water from the well.*[7]

This was an important visit since both the
Walkers and Saint-Gaudens were working on major projects Stanford White had commissioned,
such as the *Diana* sculpture, which Saint-Gaudens
was to prepare for White's Madison Square Garden
rooftop. Later, Walker was asked to participate in
the 1893 World's Columbian Exposition in
Chicago. His painting *The Gift Bearer* won a
bronze prize medal (which was designed by his
friend Saint-Gaudens). Walker's murals in the
Library of Congress and the Boston State House
were recommendations from White. Evidently,
Laura's early entertainment efforts did not deter
Mr. White from continuing his commissions with
both artists.

Evenings were a time for elaborate dinners. The
women at the head of the larger homes such as
Lydia Parrish, Adeline Adams, Annie Lazarus, Rose

(above) Lydia Parrish watching her children playing in the reflecting pool at The Oaks, circa 1916. Photo by Maxfield Parrish. Dartmouth College Library.

(left) Henry O. Walker, *The Gift Bearer*, oil on canvas, 1892. Winner of a medal at the World's Columbian Exposition, Chicago, 1893. Frame by Stanford White. Private Collection.

Nichols, and Mabel Harlakenden were witty, savvy, creative, and politically active. They used their soirees to foster personal causes, such as advancing the suffragist movement in New Hampshire and the nation and focusing the nation's attention on the masterful art being created in Cornish.

Some dinners were more eventful than others. The beautiful Lydia Parrish, Maxfield Parrish's talented wife, relates the following anecdote in her diaries dated July 28, 1906:

> *Gave a dinner for the Hapgoods, Ethel Barrymore and the Rublees and had stories on the preparation of it! Katie our cook had been like a thundercloud fighting with Sue [Lewin, the children's nanny who had just started posing for Parrish paintings]. Sue refused to do the mayonnaise and dressing. Cook said she was beginning to "put on airs" for posing for Mr. Parrish. I told her the constant quarreling in the kitchen had to stop, so she promptly gave notice just as the guests were arriving through the front door being chased in by a terrific thunderstorm. I explained the delay in the kitchen and everyone understood. We had a bully time! Later on the Churchills "butted" in as they called it be-*

fore we were through with dinner and helped keep things at a most lively pitch![8]

The curator of the Nichols House Museum in Boston's Beacon Hill told the following anecdote about Rose Nichols, whose stately home, Mastlands, now houses the Cornish Colony Museum:

> *At the turn of the century shortly after the ballroom at Mastlands had been completed, Miss Rose Nichols was giving a weekend party where a number of major artists were to be her house guests. Among them was the famous American painter John Singer Sargent, who had come in from a long sojourn in France and was visiting his friend, sculptor Augustus Saint-Gaudens, while staying in the nearby home of his niece Miss Nichols. When the notice of this appeared in the society pages of the* **Boston Globe,** *art patron Isabella Gardner, who had been soliciting Sargent's company for some time, decided to invite herself to this weekend soiree. (It was whispered that after the famous portrait of Mrs. Gardner done by the artist earlier, Jack Gardner had experienced a fit of slight jealousy. Sargent had been wisely avoiding another visit to Boston!)*

(opposite) A toast to High Court (from left: Maria Oakey Dewing, Thomas Dewing second from left, Annie Lazarus second from right, Charles Platt, right), circa 1882. Hobbs, *The Art of Thomas Wilmer Dewing*, 1996.

(above) Lydia Parrish: Shy Beauty, circa 1894. Photo by Maxfield Parrish. Dartmouth College Library.

(left) Percy MacKaye as Hermes, 1905. Photo by J. A. Thorp. Dartmouth College Library.

(right) Charlotte Houston Fairchild as a nymph, 1905. Photo by J. A. Thorp. Dartmouth College Library.

(below) Lucia Fairchild Fuller as Proserpina, 1905. Dartmouth College Library.

Mrs. Gardner (who had not been included in Miss Nichols' guest list for the weekend) sent a very imperious telegram announcing her arrival (along with members of her staff) at the White River Junction, Vermont, train station and demanding that she be met and escorted to Mastlands for the weekend.

Miss Nichols, who had plenty of starch in her own petticoats, fired back a telegram: "Oh, very well! You may attend. Just make sure that the staff you bring is your 'near and dear' since I am running out of guests rooms for this particular weekend and they will have to stay in YOUR room!" [9]

For those who stayed year-round, winter, too, brought its own measure of play, wonder, work, and contemplation. Saint-Gaudens installed a two-thousand-foot-long toboggan slide in Aspet and

encouraged many of his students and assistants to participate in winter sports on his hill. Maxfield Parrish also built a toboggan and slide for his children and tramped his woods in search of firewood and game. The light on winter mornings after a heavy snow is dazzlingly brilliant. Icicles glimmer in the snow like a thousand diamonds. It is no wonder that Willard Metcalf and Stephen and Maxfield Parrish all excelled in their creations of a winter's day light. Their depictions of Cornish's snow in either sunlight or brilliant moonlight remain hauntingly unforgettable many years after their creation.

In 1905 when Saint-Gaudens's health was failing due to cancer, the colony decided to honor him with a special fete they called "A Masque of 'Ours.'" According to Laura Walker, the idea first came about through Maxfield Parrish. Louis Shipman and Percy MacKaye wrote the play.

(above) Augustus Saint-Gaudens, circa 1905. *Cornish Celebration Presentation Plaque*, bronze, 1905. Peter and Alma Smith Collection.

(left) Hazel MacKaye as a nymph, 1905. Photo by J.A. Thorp. Dartmouth College Library.

(far left) Mrs. Percy MacKaye as Juno, 1905. Photo by J.A. Thorp. Dartmouth College Library.

Arthur Whiting composed the music and provided the orchestra, who hid among the trees in an esplanade at Aspet. A small white plaster temple was erected in the grassy esplanade.

The pageant told a story of the ancient gods and goddesses of mythology occupying the beautiful Cornish hills. Parrish played the centaur Chiron. The artist constructed an ingenious contraption of a centaur's hind legs that attached to his ankles and gave the impression of moving when he walked. Anne Parrish was Venus; Herbert Adams was Pan; Kenyon Cox, Pluto; the handsome Mrs. Winston Churchill, Diana; Ellen Shipman, the wise Minerva, and Rose Nichols was Polyhymnia.

When the gods realized that their bucolic earthly home was being taken over by mortals, they selected one among them—the sculptor Saint-Gaudens—to rule his fellow earthlings. The gods lauded Saint-Gaudens with verse and music, presented him with a golden bowl held by the Spirit of Art, proclaimed him above all others, and then drew him away in a Roman chariot.

Saint-Gaudens was emotionally touched by his friends and their love and respect. To commemorate the occasion, he cast a large bronze *Presentation Plaque*, which listed the names of all the members of the colony who had participated in "Masque of 'Ours,'" and gave each person a small silver plaquette replica as a keepsake. He died two years later, mourned and missed by all.

Spearheaded by his widow, Augusta, and their only son, Homer Saint-Gaudens, the sculptor's *Reminiscences* were published in 1913. Homer, who was assistant director of the Carnegie Institute of Art in Pittsburgh, Pennsylvania, was also founder and director of the Saint-Gaudens Memorial, now the Saint-Gaudens National Historic Site, in Cornish.

(above) Cornishites during a Fourth of July celebration, circa 1905. Photo by Maxfield Parrish. Dartmouth College Library.

(opposite) Homer and Carlota Saint-Gaudens, circa 1905. Dartmouth College Library.

CHAPTER 3

The Golden Age

*I*n their heyday, between 1900 and 1917, the towns of Cornish and Plainfield boasted a concentration of almost seventy well-known names in their rosters of summer and year-long residents. The colony's artists and writers surrounded themselves with nature's splendor, creating beautiful gardens, then captured that grandeur in their art. Art and intellectually stimulating companions set the pace in this bucolic and idyllic setting.

Perhaps no other body of work says so much about this Cornish Camelot than the murals Parrish was commissioned to paint for the Long Island studio of one of the most powerful women of that day, art patron Gertrude Vanderbilt Whitney. They spoke of an era of innocence, beauty, love, and courtship. Painted between 1914 and 1918, the murals epitomize a golden age before the First World War.

A cache of letters between members of the Parrish family that this author found hidden at The Oaks offer an insightful glimpse of this special era. In letters to his brother Dillwyn, Maxfield Parrish, Jr., writes in 1949:

> *July 4, 1949 (in a letter describing a recent visit at The Oaks):*
>
> *Trying to dissolve the haze of memories, and sort of clean off the cobwebs that obscure same. Ticklish thing, this trying to recall that Golden Age feeling, spurious, fake and possibly degenerate snobbishness though it may be, still it uplifts and makes a demigod of a plodding man. . . . A thing tasted by many of the great and near great in Cornish and not of it and will be tasted again by many in the future. . . . This Golden Age feeling . . . it is almost dangerous to feel that good.*[10]

Maxfield Parrish, *Whitney Panel One
(North Wall)*, oil on canvas, circa 1918.
Whitney Family Collection.

(below) Max Jr. gathering potatoes for the family's evening meal. Circa 1915. Photo by Maxfield Parrish. Dartmouth College Library.

(opposite) Lorraine Hapgood in the garden at High Court, circa 1905. Photo by Maxfield Parrish. Dartmouth College Library.

(below) Dillwyn and Jean Parrish in the garden at The Oaks, circa 1916. Photo by Maxfield Parrish. Dartmouth College Library.

And then again in July 29, 1949, he says,

Come to think of it us Parrish kids were a flock of the worst spoiled and more thoroughly unprepared-for-life guys you could find in a hell of a long search. The glittering Golden Age of Cornish alone is a hell of a start in life, that suckling amongst the cultural clouds of Mt. Olympus, and once out of the cradle dumped down on the earth below, naked, without weapons, cruelly spared the character building effects of work around home. True, we were disciplined, made to mind, and not allowed criminal ways to develop, but we were absolutely unprepared for life on this planet.[11]

Maxfield Parrish, Jr., later mused in another letter to his brother that psychiatrists had told him that one in ten thousand people can be considered "gifted." And Cornish and its surrounding area had more than its share of honorees.

Beloved places are also places of transition and

(below) The Oaks compound, early winter, circa 1915. Dartmouth College Library.

(above) Terraced garden at The Oaks today. Photo by David Putnam.

(right) Perennial borders at Northcote, 1999. Photo by David Putnam.

(left) Loggia and fountain at Aspet, 1999.
Photo by David Putnam.

(below) Main house at The Oaks today,
1999. Photo by David Putnam.

change—beautiful in their seasons of abundance as well as their seasons of loss. An unknown poet once said: "You never really leave a place you love. Part of it you take with you, leaving a part of yourself behind."

In Cornish, many of the artists' homes, such as The Oaks, Harlakenden, High Court, Aspet, and Mastlands, sustained damaging fires through the years that either leveled them totally or damaged them considerably. Some ruined homes have been rebuilt and restored (such as The Oaks, which this author rebuilt in 1979 and where she resides still today); like phoenixes rising from the ashes, they have survived and prospered. Some, like Harlakenden, are gone forever.

A hundred years after Saint-Gaudens first moved to Cornish, new generations of families have purchased and settled in many of the homes that the artists, sculptors, and writers once occupied. The area is no longer populated primarily by New York expatriates. The new residents come from as far away as California and as near as Massachusetts.

One common denominator appears to be the rule. The new Cornishites, although perhaps not as glittering as those who were here before and whose homes they now occupy, continue to pursue spiritual transcendence, as evidenced in their spectacular gardens.

(above) William Howard Hart, *Portrait of Mrs. Herbert Adams*, oil on canvas, 1899. George Reed and Yvonne Mathieu Collection.

(opposite) Stephen Parrish painting in his garden, 1910. Dartmouth College Library.

CHAPTER 4

Art and Artists

From 1885 to the mid-1920s the Cornish Colony saw many of the major artists, writers, jurists, and politicians of the day spend their summers in Plainfield and Cornish. The majority of these visitors were painters and sculptors.

That the artists themselves enjoyed each other's work was evident. They often purchased or traded works. Many of them, including Thomas Dewing, Maria Oakey Dewing, Edith Prellwitz, and Henry Walker, exchanged some of their paintings for one of famed architect Stanford White's elaborate frames. Frances Grimes traded Stephen Parrish her bas-relief of his niece Anne Parrish for one of Stephen Parrish's landscapes. Herbert Adams traded a marble bust to his friend William Howard Hart for a portrait of Adams's wife, Adeline.

Saint-Gaudens and Maxfield Parrish also admired each other's art. Saint-Gaudens wrote Parrish in 1901 asking about two works Parrish had executed for *Century Magazine* to illustrate John Milton's poem "L'Allegro":

> *The three drawings for Milton's Allegro you have done for the* Century *are superb and I want to tell you how they impressed me. They are big and on looking at them I felt the most choking sensation we have only in the presence of the really swell thing. . . . To whom do these things belong? Could I buy one of them? If so, I want to do so right away, quick, before some other feller gets his hands on them. . . .*[12]

ANNE·PARRISH·CORNISH·NEW·HAMPSHIRE·JVLY·M·C·M·V·

TO·STEPHEN·PARRISH·

(right) Frances Grimes, *Portrait of Anne Parrish*, marble bas-relief, 1905. U.S. Department of the Interior, National Park Service, Saint-Gaudens National Historic Site. Gift of Alma Gilbert.

(above) Augustus Saint-Gaudens's studio with plaster cast of the General Sherman sculpture, 1901. Shown are James Earle Fraser (second from left), Saint-Gaudens (third from left), Henry Hering (fifth from left), and Elsie Ward (right). Dartmouth College Library.

The paintings had been promised to another art collector, and Parrish, although flattered because he sincerely respected and loved the sculptor, was unable to provide him with the desired objects. Five years later, Parrish wrote Saint-Gaudens in July 28, 1906:

And now another matter which for pure impertinence and morbid lack of delicacy I fear you will consider the limit. I see on the market bronze miniatures of your works, and what I want to know is this: is it possible to buy a plaster cast original size of the round Stevenson? I have had a hanker for this particular one for years and years, and in spite of almost super human efforts to live it down, it simply grows and grows.

We are building a big room which when finished is going to make the Apollo gallery in the Louvre look like a waiting room in a railway station. That's where I have dreamed of putting it. I had planned to put the Sherman at one end,

but I find the room is just four inches too narrow. [Author's note: Parrish is jokingly referring to the fifteen-foot-high sculpture of General William Tecumseh Sherman at the entrance of Central Park in Fifth Avenue, New York City.]

Sometimes in a lucid interval tell me to go to hell on a post card: and I will understand perfectly. Nerve is its own reward. You ought to see me at work on the big picture: below is a tracing from a photograph showing relative size of me and it. Our best to you, Maxfield Parrish.[13]

Evidently the sculptor was pleased that Parrish in turn coveted one of his works. The largest of Saint-Gaudens's casts of the famous portrait, measuring three feet in diameter, was sent to Parrish as a gift, a token of Saint-Gaudens's appreciation for Parrish's kindness during the sculptor's illness.

Besides Saint-Gaudens, other sculptors that energized the Cornish Colony were Herbert Adams,

Maxfield Parrish, *Poet's Dream*, oil on paper, 1901. Private Collection.

Maxfield Parrish, sketch for a mural on letter to Augustus Saint-Gaudens. July 28, 1906. Dartmouth College Library.

Clockwise from top left.

Herbert Adams, *Flora*, bronze sculpture, 1929. Private Collection. Courtesy of Peter S. Nyboer.

Herbert Adams, *Infant Burbank*, bronze fountain head, 1905. Private Collection. Courtesy of Peter S. Nyboer.

Daniel Chester French, *Victory: Model for the First Division Memorial*, gilded bronze, 1921-24. Peter and Alma Smith Collection.

Frederic Remington, *Coming Through the Rye*, authorized posthumous bronze, Roman Bronze Works, New York, 1933. Peter and Alma Smith Collection.

Frederic Remington, Frances Grimes, Louis and Annetta St. Gaudens, James Earle Fraser, Frederic MacMonnies, Paul Manship, and, of course, Daniel Chester French. Many of the sculptors and painters had first met each other while visiting or working in the Paris salons and then renewed their acquaintances in the thriving and competitive New York galleries.

Art historians are divided as to which sculptor was the most influential during the early part of the century: Saint-Gaudens or French. Saint-Gaudens, a permanent founding member of the Cornish Colony, certainly influenced MacMonnies, Grimes, and Fraser, who worked as his assistants. He un-doubtedly also influenced the sculpture of Remington and Adams, who came to his studio and exchanged ideas. Although Saint-Gaudens and French saw each other as friendly competitors, it was French's influence and his standing with the Metropolitan Museum of Art's board of directors that earned Saint-Gaudens a place there. French signaled the end of the age of innocence with his somber but spectacular *Victory: The First Division Memorial*, which he executed in 1921 as a testimony for those soldiers who did not return from the hor-rors of World War I. It is amazing to ponder the breadth of the sculptures that emanated from or had their start in Cornish.

Maxfield Parrish collaborated with Louis Comfort Tiffany on the spectacular *Dream Garden* mosaic (1916), a fifty-foot-long work of art in-spired and based on Parrish's own garden at The Oaks. This shimmering creation, containing close to a million pieces of glass, is the only one of its kind in this country.

In Edward Bok's book, *The Americanization of Edward Bok*, the famed Curtis Publishing executive relates how the world-renowned Parrish/Tiffany mosaic at the entry of the Curtis Building in Philadelphia's Independence Square came about.

Bok recalled that one day while at Maxfield Parrish's home in New Hampshire the artist had told him of a dream garden which he would like to construct, not on canvas but in reality. Bok suggested to Parrish that he come to New York. He asked him if he could put his dream garden on canvas. The artist thought he could; in fact, was greatly attracted to the idea; but he knew nothing of mosaic work…Bok took Parrish to Mr. Tiffany's studio, the two artists talked to-gether and the wonder-picture in glass of which painters had declared that "mere words are only aggravating in describing this amazing picture" became a reality.[14]

The Dream Garden was the collaboration of two of the most important artists of their day. This work was the first American artwork designated an his-toric art object (July 1998) and worthy of historic preservation.

Art engenders art. The inspiration and the syn-ergy created in the artists' colony were without par. Many of the artists had dual disciplines. Remington, Fraser, MacMonnies, and French were not only sculptors of note, they were also painters.

Although French was only a summer resident at the colony during 1891 and 1893, it was in Cornish that his painting and sketching really took

(right) Stephen Parrish and his sketching class, circa 1890. Dartmouth College Library.

(below) Maxfield Parrish and Louis Comfort Tiffany, *Dream Garden*, mosaic executed in favrile glass, 1915. Collection of the estate of John W. Merriam.

hold, as evidenced in the haunting pastel portrait of his wife and daughter done in Cornish in 1893. According to Wanda Styka of the Daniel Chester French Museum in Stockbridge, Massachusetts, French used his drawing and painting time to relax after a day of sculpting. Perhaps it was in Cornish that his interest in other art forms began. The inscription on Daniel Chester French's tomb in Concord's Sleepy Hollow Cemetery states his name, dates, and a simple phrase, the credo of his life: "A Heritage of Beauty."

Two artists that received international recognition with their paintings and etchings were Stephen Parrish and his pupil Charles Platt. Their etchings rival another contemporary, James McNeill Whistler (1834–1903). Stephen taught etching in Philadelphia and brought that discipline to Cornish. Platt found etching enormously interesting and became quite accomplished under Parrish's influence.

Writers such as Winston Churchill and art historian and critic Adeline Pond Adams dabbled in painting and politics. Churchill ran for state office. Adams was a leader in the local suffragist movement.

Maxfield Parrish collaborated with Louise Saunders (Scribner editor Maxwell Perkins's wife) on her great children's classic *Knave of Hearts*. Saunders rented Rose Nichols's home, Mastlands, because of its proximity to The Oaks and Parrish, who was illustrating her book.

Louis and Ellen Shipman were noted locally not only for their participation in life at the colony, but also for their contributions to local gardens. Ellen Shipman, in fact, later became a well-known garden designer. Rose Nichols also became a garden designer and wrote three books and many articles on gardening. Rose invited many stellar figures from the worlds of art, politics, and literature to her soirees on a porch overlooking her masterful gardens. Politicians, presidents, artists, queens, and

(above) Stephen Parrish, *Fecamp*, etching, 1880. Peter and Alma Smith Collection.

(above) Charles A. Platt, *Dry Goods Store*, etching, 1881. Peter and Alma Smith Collection.

(left) Winston Churchill, *Mrs. Spaulding's House*, watercolor, circa 1913. Peter and Alma Smith Collection.

(above) Maxfield Parrish, *Daybreak*, oil on board, 1923. Private Collection.

(right) Willard Metcalf, *In the Garden*, oil on canvas, 1878. Peter and Alma Smith Collection.

(right) Charles A. Platt garden with brick walkways and planted urns, 1999. Photo by David Putnam.

(below) William Henry Hyde, *Landscape in Cornish*, oil on canvas, circa 1908. Peter and Alma Smith Collection.

courtesans were all welcome at her home and gardens, provided they brought the gift of conversation or witty repartee with them!

The names at the colony represent an honor guard of the artists, writers, and garden designers who dedicated their lives to the pursuit and depiction of beauty during the American Renaissance of art. Maxfield Parrish painted *Daybreak* at Cornish in 1923, which became the most reproduced work in the history of art. Important political decisions were discussed and enacted in Cornish as well.

Word of the Cornish Colony spread among the nation's art community. Artists came to see and paint the surrounding country. The natural splendor challenged and inspired them to portray the sky's indescribable color, the colors of the gardens, winter's shimmering snow, or the Connecticut River reflect-

ing a bridge or a church's spires. Whether in paint, sculpture, prose, poetry, or the wondrous mixes of texture and color in a garden, the colony's artists shared their glimpse of beauty with all of us.

A visitor to the Cornish Colony Museum recently told this author that genius creates a vortex that attracts people, almost magnetically, to its center: a strong, gravitational pull that cannot be ignored. History bears out the colony's lure in the fecundity of talent that prospered in Cornish. The many artworks and the fantastic gardens live on today, a legacy of beauty that we may still experience and enjoy.

II

The Gardens of the Cornish Colony

by Judith B. Tankard

(above) Augusta Saint-Gaudens on the upper terrace of the flower gardens at Aspet, circa 1906. Dartmouth College Library.

(left) Loggia at High Court with vista of Ascutney in background, 1999. Photo by David Putnam.

CHAPTER 5

A History of the Cornish Gardens

What made the gardens of the Cornish Colony so special? The most obvious answer is that the gardens, the flowers in them, and the views out provided subject matter for paintings by Winston Churchill, Maria Oakey Dewing, Frances Houston, William Hyde, Maxfield and Stephen Parrish, Charles Platt, and other artists. Today these works of art provide delicious mementos of Cornish gardens as they were a hundred years ago. Mattie Edwards Hewitt's photographs, commissioned in 1923 for *House and Garden* magazine, captured many of the gardens at the height of their maturity. Multitalented Maxfield Parrish took photographs of his own garden at The Oaks and his father's garden at Northcote. The Shipmans, like other Cornish families, took snapshots of their houses and gardens. The artwork and the photographs provide an extraordinary visual record of luscious historic gardens in their prime.

Despite the undeniable genius of the artistic creations produced by Cornish Colony's residents, it was the artists' gardens rather than their inspired works of art that earned Cornish its national reputation. It was no wonder, since the colony was richly embroidered with storybook gardens filled with old-fashioned flowers and quaint outdoor furnishings.

For many of the colony's artists, garden making was an intellectually absorbing pastime. Because of the artists' training in the visual arts, their gardens were planned with a deep

(opposite) Dingleton House gardens, 1923. Photo by Mattie Edwards Hewitt. Shelton, *Beautiful Gardens in America*, 1924.

(top) An award-winning garden in the Mothers' and Daughters' Club annual competition in Plainfield, circa 1930. Plainfield Historical Society.

The richly planted Italian Garden at Dingleton House framed by a pergola and latticework. Photo by Mattie Edwards Hewitt. Shelton, *Beautiful Gardens in America*, 1924.

knowledge of design principles and artistic judgment. Where else, except Italy, could one find so
many delightful country gardens that married
house and garden to the site so successfully?

Endless hours were spent lavishing care on gardens, visiting one another's gardens, and exchang-
ing lore at frequent dinner parties. The fever pitch
was such that one resident artist commented: "One
night when a number of us were dining with
Maxfield Parrish, the talk had been so continually
upon plants and diseases that he rose, put his hands
on the table, leaned over, and said in a deep voice,
'Let us spray.'"[1] The strong sense of camaraderie
and community spirit in Cornish infused
Cornishites with the energy needed to deal with

the climate, to combat pests, and to face all the
other trials and tribulations of gardening.

The colony's letter writers and diarists, such as
Frances Grimes, Stephen Parrish, Augustus Saint-
Gaudens, Margaret Shurcliff, Laura Walker, and
First Lady Ellen Wilson, provide glimpses of life in
the colony, including praise for one another's gardens. The competition must have been keen as to
who had the most beautiful, best considered garden. Ellen Axson Wilson (the first Mrs. Woodrow
Wilson, who died in 1914) wrote rapturous letters
back home to the President in Washington during
the summer of 1913 describing her busy social
schedule that included sitting for her portrait by
Robert Vonnoh. She thought all the gardens lovely

(above) The Oaks, home of Lydia and Maxfield Parrish, as pictured in Duncan's article. *Century Magazine*, 1906.

(left) Robert Vonnoh, *Mrs. Woodrow Wilson and Her Three Daughters*, oil on canvas, 1913. Woodrow Wilson House, Washington, D.C.

(below) Henry O. Walker's house, designed by Charles Platt in 1890. *Century Magazine*, 1906.

in their own way: "Mrs. Shipman's garden is one of the most beautiful in its solid masses of bloom," while Maxfield Parrish's was "a delightful tangle" and Howard Hart's was "one of the prettiest" for its simplicity.[2]

Pride in gardening was so ingrained in the community spirit that in the 1930s Ellen Shipman, under the auspices of the Mothers' and Daughters' Club, annually sponsored a competition among homeowners in Plainfield, awarding a prize to the one with the best garden (glass slides of the prize-winning gardens are held at the Plainfield Historical Society). In 1914, Lydia Parrish helped children in the area to plan and maintain school gardens by awarding a prize for the best gardens.

Garden journalist Frances Duncan, who spent many summers in Cornish, was among the first to bring the high level of gardening arts in the colony to national attention. In 1905, *Century Magazine* sent her to Cornish to write about Maxfield Parrish's house and garden, then in its formative stages. Parrish was the man of the moment—he had recently illustrated Edith Wharton's *Italian Villas and Their Gardens* (1904) with enchanting views of classic gardens. The following year Duncan wrote about other gardens in the colony, citing those of Winston Churchill, Kenyon Cox, Herbert Croly, Maria and Thomas Dewing, Frances Houston, Rose Nichols, Stephen Parrish, Maxfield Parrish, Charles Platt, Louis Shipman, and Henry O. Walker.

(right) Howard Hart's garden with perennial borders and hedging. Herbert Adams's studio is just visible on the right. Photo by Ellen Shipman. Courtesy of Nancy Angell Streeter.

(below) The garden at Crossways, 1999. Photo by Judith B. Tankard

Duncan deemed Cornish "one of the most hopeful spots [to witness] the future of American garden art," praising its consistently high level of achievements.[3] In contrast to the more pretentious estates that were proliferating across America in the early 1900s, Duncan applauded the colony's well-conceived, simple homes and gardens that were always subordinate to views that could be enjoyed from them. "A garden is not sacred and a thing apart, to be gazed at from the drawing room windows or strolled through occasionally with an admiring visitor. It is simply an outgrowth of the house…to be used and changed if one pleases, until one finds the best possible arrangement," she wrote.[4] Duncan particularly extolled Stephen Parrish's and Rose Standish Nichols's gardens, two of the colony's outstanding creations, in later articles. She had planned a story on the Saint-Gaudens's garden, but the sculptor, who was in failing health and soon to die, valued his privacy.[5]

Aspet, the home of Augusta and Augustus Saint-Gaudens, is the most visible garden in the colony today. For many years it provided visual refreshment for the family and a beautiful setting for communal activities, such as masques and picnics. The gardens slowly evolved from simple flower borders to sophisticated settings for sculpture, in keeping with the colony's other gardens. Recently restored by the National Park Service, which has administered the property since 1965, the gardens bring pleasure to countless visitors each year.

Not all of the colony's gardens have survived intact to the extent that Aspet has. In some cases the outlines of old gardens provide the framework for new ones, such as Thomas and Maria Dewings' Doveridge. Among the earliest and most elaborate, the Dewings' garden can be relived in the artists' paintings—Thomas's ethereal landscapes depicting

the Cornish fields and hills, Maria's vibrant floral compositions filled with flowers from her garden.

Portrait painter Frances C. Houston's charming hillside garden at Crossways has recently been cleared and replanted. At one time, a white-painted fence of Thomas Dewing's design enclosed it on the front side, with a pair of pyramidal arborvitae (*Thuja occidentalis*) flanking the gate. A small reflecting pool in the center and a long, curved bench (or exedra) sheltered under pine trees provided the architectural elements for a dense flower garden. Iron poles, set out at intervals to encourage climbers, defined one side of the garden, while the other, facing a steep drop in the ground, was defined by a long stone wall. Like Maria Dewing's garden, Frances Houston's was planted with an eye for painting. "The studio wall is radiant with *Clematis paniculata*, and against the porch grows a lusty gray-green honeysuckle with excellent effect," wrote Frances Duncan.[6] Another writer thought it "perhaps the most charming old-fashioned garden in Cornish."[7]

Artist William Howard Hart's house and garden have long since disappeared. A landscape and portrait painter as well as a stage designer (he founded the Howard Hart Players), Hart was an avid gardener. Because he lived just up the hill from his friend, the sculptor Herbert Adams, also an avid gardener, there was always a sense of friendly competition between the two. Ellen Shipman's snapshots of Hart's house and garden show neatly edged flower beds filled with perennials and clumps of shrubbery on the lawn. His old New England farmhouse, which he left to Adams, was later torn down and the garden demolished.

Stephen Parrish stands out as the most passionate of all the colony's gardeners. "Landscape painter for the fun of it [he was] a gardener for the love of it," quipped one writer.[8] Northcote, his hilltop

(left) Maria Oakey Dewing, *Irises and Calla Lilies*, oil on panel, circa 1890–1905. Detroit Institute of Arts, Founders Society Purchase, Dexter M. Ferry Jr. Fund.

(above) Frances Houston's hillside garden. *Century Magazine*, 1906.

(left) A long semicircular bench and small reflecting pool at Crossways. Photo by Jessie Tarbox Beals. Shelton, *Beautiful Gardens in America*, 1915.

(opposite) Solid masses of bloom in Ellen Shipman's garden at Brook Place, 1923. Photo Mattie Edwards Hewitt. Courtesy of Nancy Angell Streeter.

(right) Maxfield Parrish, *Land of Make-Believe*, oil on canvas, 1905. Private Collection. Photo Alma Gilbert Collection.

(below) Rose Nichols's walled garden, with flower borders and benches encircling a pool and Mount Ascutney in the background. Lowell, *American Gardens*, 1902.

home overlooking the Connecticut River Valley, was both highly considered and expansively planted. Parrish's diaries detailing his annual struggle with winter-kill and summer pests, and the never-ending flow of ideas that shaped his garden, provide a vivid picture of what gardening was all about in the colony. Dozens of nostalgic photographs of Northcote, taken by Parrish himself or by his son Fred (better known as Maxfield), help bring to life again the essence of Cornish gardening at its best. Recently restored, the garden reveals the layers of Parrish's ingenuity.

Maxfield Parrish was bitten by the gardening passion in a different way. The dreamlike setting of his home, The Oaks, was known the world over in his magazine covers, calendar art, and book illustrations. Perched on a hill in Plainfield, The Oaks still commands one of the most spectacular views in the area. Parrish conceived his highly individualistic gardens as a series of "rooms" for framing the view to Mount Ascutney.

While the Dewings introduced flower gardening to Cornish, the person most responsible for molding the colony's rich design heritage was Charles Adams Platt, the etcher and later landscape

painter who turned to garden design and architecture during his formative years while summering in the colony. Few architects or designers have surpassed Platt in his ability to so fully integrate house, garden, and landscape into one harmonious whole. Basing his design principles on his deep understanding of Italian villas, Platt sought to create distinctive houses suited to the needs of Americans. His widely known commissions at High Court, Dingleton House, and his own house—still considered the architectural jewels of the colony— brought him national recognition as an architect.

Platt's mentoring of the colony's two distinguished professional garden designers—Rose Standish Nichols and Ellen Biddle Shipman— spread his ideas farther afield, but in different ways. Rose Nichols responded to her study of English and Italian formal gardens. Her large (overly large, in fact) walled garden in the colony, outlined with hand-built rustic stone walls, was more formal in spirit than many of her neighbors' hillside gardens. Other than its flower-bejeweled borders, it lacked the artist-inspired furnishings so characteristic of the colony's other gardens.

Ellen Shipman fully embraced the colony's aes-

(left) A classic dooryard garden on Long Island, designed by Ellen Shipman, 1923. Photo Mattie Edwards Hewitt. Rare and Manuscripts Collection, Cornell University Library.

(below) The main path in Stephen Parrish's garden, with a lily pool on axis with the house, 1898. Alma Gilbert Collection.

Grapevines covering the loggia at Brook Place, 1923. Photo by Mattie Edwards Hewitt. Courtesy of Nancy Angell Streeter.

thetic at Brook Place, where luscious plantings and countrified embellishments took precedence over a modest layout. Shipman's knack for making the garden outlines disappear with artfully layered plantings made her one of the most highly sought-after landscape architects in the country during the 1920s. Her signature style, based on her intimate knowledge of Cornish gardens, revolved around an unpretentious layout, generous amounts of background greenery, lush plantings, and well-placed garden ornament.

While Charles Platt's artistic eye brought an undeniable sophistication to the Cornish Colony, the colony also owes its debt to traditional New England dooryard gardens. These were characterized by floral abundance and an overwhelming sense of domesticity, with ambiance the single most important quality. They were never meant to impress anyone, but were havens of peace and repose, a place to collect one's thoughts after a hard day's work. In the words of Duncan, they exuded "a certain quality of homelikeness." [9] In many ways, Stephen Parrish's Northcote best exemplifies this ideal. Artfully laid out and beautifully planted, it had an overall feeling of repose rather than being dominated by design.

Ellen Shipman, who translated the dooryard garden into a heavenly, plant-intensive haven, recalled in later years that for her, Cornish represented "the renaissance of gardening in America, the first effort in this country to return to early traditional gardening." [10] She was referring to the explosion of interest in gardens in the late nineteenth

century, as people turned away from the Victorian era's aesthetic of flower beds filled with brightly colored seasonal annuals and instead looked back to the colonial era for inspiration. Paintings and photographs of these nostalgic gardens (now known as colonial revival gardens), showing picket fences, garden arbors, and boxwood-edged flower beds with clusters of billowing plants, filled the pages of periodicals and books at the turn of the century. Some books—such as Helena Rutherfurd Ely's *The Woman's Hardy Garden* (1903), Alice Morse Earle's *Old-Time Gardens* (1901) and *Sun-Dials and Roses of Yesterday* (1902), and Mable Osgood Wright's *The Garden You and I* (1906)—were aimed specifically at women and their gardening needs.

Using the colonial dooryard garden as a starting point, Cornishites outlined the garden enclosure with a wall, fence, or a hedge to bring it into close proximity with the house. Straight paths on axis with the house, usually with a central pool, fountain, sundial, or other special feature to mark the convergence of paths, lent symmetry to the composition. Rectangular beds edged with plank boards rather than a crisper, more formal edging such as stone, lent informality. Arbors were smothered with grapevines or roses and a bench set out under a shady tree. *Berberis vulgaris*, *Spiraea prunifolia*, mock orange (*Philadelphus coronarius*), and common lilacs were staple shrubs, while highly colored ornamental trees, such as maples, variegated evergreens, and "showy" plants, such as cannas or crimson rambler roses, were generally eschewed.

While home gardeners such as Stephen Parrish

(right) Hardy phlox in a Cornish garden. Photo Ellen Shipman. Courtesy of Nancy Angell Streeter.

(below) Cascades of spirea at The Oaks. Alma Gilbert Collection.

(right) A Lombardy poplar, with Mount Ascutney in the background, at Aspet, circa 1907. Dartmouth College Library.

(above) Hollyhocks in Stephen Parrish's garden at Northcote, 1898. Dartmouth College Library.

View from the terrace at Charles Platt's place, 1923. Photo Mattie Edwards Hewitt. Courtesy of members of the Platt family.

were more likely to respond to the American flower garden aesthetic, architects and professional garden designers turned to England and Italy for design inspiration. As Rose Nichols first pointed out, Cornish gardeners became champions of the formal school of garden design based on their assiduous study of books that were being published in England at that time. John Sedding's *Garden Craft Old and New* (1891) and Reginald Blomfield's *The Formal Garden in England* (1892) advocated an axial garden layout, with linear paths and architectural embellishments, as opposed to the more naturalistic, horticulturally inclined school promoted by William Robinson and Gertrude Jekyll.

Evidence of the colony's inclination to the formal school of design shows up in the use of a geometric layout and clipped hedges to create outdoor "garden rooms." Planters filled with hydrangeas or clipped evergreens, and set out at strategic points, strengthened the geometric layout. These are evident in all of Platt's Cornish gardens. In place of massive olive jars, urns, and large tubs with laurel trees that dominated Italianate gardens (including Platt's larger commissions elsewhere), small terra-cotta pots with peony standards were used to great effect.

The New Hampshire climate was not exactly ideal for gardening—the summers were hot and dry and the first frost came all too soon. The colony's gardeners had to work hard to find plants that were hardy to their climate while artistically acceptable. Boxwood, privet, and other traditional kinds of hedging did not fare well in New Hampshire, especially if they were not protected. In their place, Cornishites had great success with pine, Japanese barberry, and the ubiquitous *Spiraea* x *vanhouttei* as clipped hedges. Lombardy poplars (*Populus nigra* 'Italica'), a fast-growing, but disease-prone tree, can be found in many Cornish gardens. Their columnar shape added a touch of the Italian hills to the Cornish hills. Maxfield Parrish wisely decided against using them at The Oaks where they would have been dwarfed among the towering oaks that distinguished the site.

Above all, a profusion of flowers lingers most in our memory of historic Cornish gardens. "When I first planted my garden," said Herbert Adams, "I thought I liked some flowers better than others; but, after you've worked among flowers awhile, no matter what kind of flowers they are, you like them. I've noticed that certain flowers grow better for

(right) Maxfield Parrish, *Agib in the Enchanted Palace*, glazed oil on paper, circa 1905. Detroit Institute of Arts, bequest of the estate of Dollie May Fisher. Parrish's painting with a mirror pool, urns, spirea, and towering trees is a fanciful version of The Oaks.

some people than for others. There's William Howard Hart—anything will grow for him! When I asked him the secret of his success, he just held up his grubbing fork."[11]

Both Rose Nichols and Stephen Parrish chronicled their difficulties in getting specific plants to perform at the right time in the right place, the woe of gardeners worldwide. Hollyhocks, iris, larkspurs, monkshood, oriental poppies, peonies, hardy phlox, and *Rosa rugosa* quickly became staples of Cornish gardens because they responded to the climate. Since most of the artists did not arrive in Cornish until the early summer, spring bulbs were generally uncommon.

In addition to the distinctive layout and planting of Cornish gardens, another integral element was "those little touches which no one but an artist would have thought of perpetrating. . . . a few columns, a stone floor against the house, and an amphora or a colored relief . . . one might have been in Italy."[12]   Terra-cotta pots and large decorative urns, such as those depicted in Maxfield Parrish's paintings, lent a certain panache to the composition. Loggias swathed in grapevines provided a pleasant frame for the picture as well as background color and texture. Examples of garden craft ranged from classical-inspired pergolas, loggias, arbors, and trellises to rustic country benches and gates. From Platt-designed loggias to quaint gates made in the home workshop or by local carpenters, each structure served a purpose in the garden. The signature circular pool found in numerous Cornish gardens, such as Charles Platt's and Stephen Parrish's, is preserved in Maxfield Parrish's painting *Agib in the Enchanted Palace*.

Frances Grimes considered sculpture "the one important thing, everything else was in another sphere of interest and subordinate."[13]   Whether

(left) Mirror pool at High Court, 1999. Photo David Putnam.

(below) Custom-built garden bench at High Court, 1999. Photo David Putnam.

brought back from Europe or cast in a Cornish studio, sculptural pieces were an important component of garden design in the colony. Aspet, which still boasts the most extensive collection of garden sculpture in the colony, incorporates casts of antique figures as well as examples of the sculptor's own work. Herbert Adams's courtyard garden, with twin hermes on pedestals marking the studio entrance, was expressly conceived to display sculpture. Many colonists featured Adams' sculptural pieces in their gardens. Ellen Shipman helped spread the renown of the colony's artists in her signature use of figurative pieces by Herbert Adams and Louis St. Gaudens (brother of Augustus Saint-Gaudens) in her commissions from New England to Northern Ohio.

Above all, the charm of Cornish gardens was the way they blended the informal plantings of dooryard gardens with formal design principles. Each one was an individual response to this aesthetic, whether a painter's garden filled with a riot of colorful flowers or an architect's manipulation of the overpowering view to Mount Ascutney. Each one was thoughtfully designed, planted, and decorated to reflect the owner's personality. No two were alike, but they all had common bonds.

A visual tour of some of the colony's exceptional historic gardens provides an opportunity to revisit many described by Frances Duncan and other period writers. While some gardens have disappeared and others have been modified over the years, as many have been carefully maintained or re-created. As they were a hundred years ago, most Cornish gardens are still private. In 1914 Charles Platt admitted to a journalist that he somewhat regretted that the gardens of the colony had become so famous that people actually traveled from afar to see them. "People come in their automobiles and their carriages, and everything you can think of, and when you have a little two-by-four piece of ground that you work in yourself, you don't like to have everybody standing around looking at you."[14] Keeping that in mind, visitors are invited to enjoy the magnificent scenery that the colony affords and pay a visit to the Cornish Colony Gallery and Museum, the Saint-Gaudens National Historic Site, and local historical societies. A number of private gardens featured in this book are occasionally open for annual tours sponsored by Historic Windsor, Inc. See the Resources section at the back of the book for further information about visiting some of these gardens.

(above) Augustus Saint-Gaudens looking out of the Little Studio, August
1906. Dartmouth College Library.

(opposite top) The New Gallery, 1999.
Photo by David Putnam.

Aspet: A Sculptor's Garden

> The home of the late Augustus Saint-Gaudens…commands one of the loveliest prospects imaginable and contains, in its unaffected lines and simple surfaces, a quiet and appealing beauty.
>
> —*House and Garden, May 1924*

If it had not been for the foresight of Augusta Saint-Gaudens (1848–1926) when she first set eyes on Huggins' Folly in 1885, the Cornish Colony might not have been born. When she and her husband, the sculptor Augustus Saint-Gaudens (1843–1907), were "casting about for a summer residence," they visited Cornish at the invitation of Charles C. Beaman, the convivial New York attorney who had acquired much of the land and farmhouses in the area and is credited with founding the colony. When Beaman offered the Saint-Gaudenses a Dutch-gabled eighteenth-century inn that had seen better days, Augustus was tempted to flee at once. But Augusta could envision happy days ahead and convinced her husband to rent it.

At that time Saint-Gaudens's reputation was just emerging; he was thirty-seven years old and had recently completed the Farragut Monument in Madison Square Park. He would later become famous for his gilded Diana atop Madison Square Garden and the somber Shaw Memorial in Boston. He was probably the most respected sculptor of his generation, and his presence in the colony was the magnet that drew other artists. Saint-Gaudens was delighted by the prevailing summer breezes and dramatic views in Cornish, so reminiscent of

(right) Edith Prellwitz, *Saint-Gaudens Garden*, oil on canvas, 1898. U.S. Department of the Interior, National Park Service, Saint-Gaudens National Historical Site, Cornish, N.H.

(below) The attractive colonnaded porch at Aspet, 1999. Photo by David Putnam.

Italy, where he had trained. Beaman's land had a magnificent view overlooking the Connecticut River Valley and a delightful rushing brook called Blow-Me-Down Brook, which lent the name Blowmeup to the property. It was a cool and delightful spot, far away from Saint-Gaudens's hot studio in New York City.

Six years later, Saint-Gaudens, wanting to do some improvements, purchased the house, outbuildings, and eighty-three acres of land from Beaman for $2,500 plus a bas-relief portrait of Beaman. Saint-Gaudens promptly renamed his new house Aspet, after his father's birthplace in France, and commissioned architect George Fletcher Babb to transform the bleak and austere house into something more charming, commanding him to "make this house smile."[15] Smile it did, by the addition of a wide-columned porch, new bedrooms, and numerous aesthetic improvements, including whitewashing the brick. In 1904 Babb built a studio on the site of the old barn to harmonize with the house, incorporating a sixty-foot pergola with Doric columns, red stucco walls, and casts from the Parthenon frieze to give it a Mediterranean flair. Babb also rebuilt the Little Studio (or Studio of the Pergola), which today houses a display of the sculp-

tor's works. Saint-Gaudens's other studio (known as the Studio of the Caryatids), where he cast larger pieces, was destroyed by fire in 1944 and replaced with a New Gallery, now an exhibition space for the Saint-Gaudens National Historic Site.

Saint-Gaudens directed his artistic energy to the layout of the garden, while Augusta, who can be seen in many photographs, was the principal caretaker for years, especially after her husband's death. Whether his favorite niece, Rose Standish Nichols, had any input on the garden is unknown, but Margaret Nichols Shurcliff (Rose's youngest sister) fondly remembered "Uncle Gus":

Uncle Augustus took a great deal of joy in landscaping the grounds, and was the first to plant rows and rows of pine hedges. He surrounded the flower garden, the vegetable garden, the clothes yard and the swimming pool with pine hedges, thickened with a few scattered hemlocks. Like many a genius, Uncle Augustus was never satisfied. He was always rearranging his sculpture and he liked to rearrange the hedges. Mr. Sears, a local farmer with a gift for transplanting, did not always see eye to eye with Uncle Augustus when he ordered one of these arbitrary upheavals. Mr. Sears

Rose Nichols, Frances Grimes, and Augusta Saint-Gaudens seated in the lily garden, circa 1900. Clipped white pine hedges form the background. Dartmouth College Library.

remonstrated that it was only last fall he had carefully planted the hedge by the garden and it was growing well; what sense was there in digging it up again? Uncle Augustus, who had a very gentle, self-derogatory disposition, did not enjoy trying to back up his whims with reason. The only way to handle Mr. Sears . . . was to begin by saying, "You know, Mr. Sears, I change my mind so often you must think I am unreasonable; in fact I think I am a little daffy. You will just have to treat me as if I were and never argue with me."[16]

Saint-Gaudens located the garden on the gently sloping ground between the house and the studio. At first there was a lily garden with a small pool, enclosed by high clipped hedges of Eastern White pine (*Pinus strobus*) and hemlock (now over one hundred years old). The hedging provided privacy and a theatrical backdrop for the flowers. Edith Prellwitz's painting, *Saint-Gaudens Garden*, shows this delightful garden with its simple, old-fashioned flower borders and pool that were signatures of Cornish gardens. Clumps of white birch trees provided a sparkling contrast with the dark green hedges. He added Lombardy poplars to flank the terrace of the house and a thornless honey locust that still shades the front entrance today.

Around 1904, after the Saint-Gaudenses gave up their New York City home and moved to the colony permanently because of Augustus's failing

(left) Piping Pan under the shadows of Mount Ascutney, 1999. Photo by Judith B. Tankard.

(below) The middle terrace at Aspet, 1999. Photo by David Putnam.

health, the sculptor decided to rework his garden into the basic layout that can be seen today. He even engaged a photographer to document various mock-ups of architectural features, such as an arbor, before rejecting them or installing them in the garden. He broke the garden area into three terraces, creating a large rectangular-shaped outdoor room. The attractive white balustrade fence that surrounds the house was continued onto the terraces to reinforce the intimacy between house and garden in the same way that the vine-covered porch does.

On the upper terrace, he devised dense flower beds with brick steps leading down to the middle terrace, the largest of the three, with the tiny pool surrounded by more flowers. The lower terrace, enclosed by three walls of hedge, was a secluded area. Most of the plants on the terraces were old-fashioned varieties, such as white, pink, and wine-red peonies and scarlet poppies. In midsummer the garden was filled with delphinium, hollyhock, gypsophila, phlox, lilies, and the like.

The garden is ingeniously designed so that a visitor feels as if he has stepped from the house into an outdoor parlor decked out with "furnishings." In addition to the pool from the former lily garden, Saint-Gaudens incorporated an array of statuary, such as the gilded antique figure of Hermes, that linger among the flowers. In the courtyard adjacent to the Little Studio, a gilded Pan overlooks a rectangular marble pool with bronze fish fountains. A long, wooden bench (or exedra) in the Pan garden has end panels cast by Louis St. Gaudens and another bench on the lower terrace has zodiac heads flanking either side. Similar exedra appear in the gardens at High Court. In the end, the elegant garden surrounding the gaunt house caused one acquaintance to suggest that the house, surrounded by such an elegant garden, looked like "a New England old maid struggling in the arms of a satyr."[17]

Augusta Saint-Gaudens, with arbor mock-up in background, 1904. Dartmouth College Library.

Considering that the garden has been in continuous existence for over a hundred years, it has undergone numerous changes. After the sculptor's death in 1907, Augusta took care of the garden until her death in 1926. Many changes came about during the era of the Saint-Gaudens Memorial, which Augusta and their son, Homer, had established to preserve the site. When Mattie Edwards Hewitt came to Cornish in 1923, she photographed Aspet's gardens in their lush maturity.[18] In 1928, Ellen Shipman, who was a devoted trustee of the Memorial, was asked to refurbish the plantings that had become dense and were out of date in style. There is no evidence that she advised on the gardens prior to that date. She drew up plans to simplify the middle terrace again in 1941. With a masterly hand, she introduced better-performing perennials, while keeping the garden "as Saint-Gaudens knew and loved it."[19]

Today the gardens have attractive double borders filled with sun-loving perennials on the upper and middle terraces, and shade-loving plants on the lower level. Hardy delphinium, hollyhocks, peonies, iris, astilbes, lady's mantle, hostas, and daylilies form the core of the plantings. Towering hollyhocks bloom beneath the vine-covered Little Studio pergola. The garden receives loving care under the aegis of the National Park Service, whose goal is to maintain the ambiance of Saint-Gaudens's day. It is open to the public year-round.

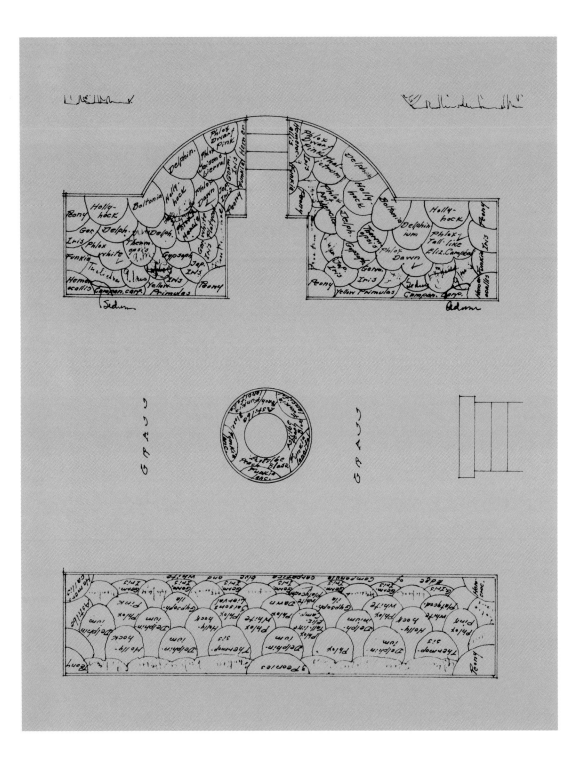

(opposite) Ellen Shipman's planting plan for the middle terrace, 1941. Rare and Manuscripts Collection, Cornell University Library.

(above) The terrace gardens during the Saint-Gaudens Memorial era, 1923. Photo by Mattie Edwards Hewitt. Shelton, *Beautiful Gardens in America*, 1924.

(left) Hermes lingers in the perennial borders, 1999. Photo David Putnam.

(above) The Dewings' garden. *Century Magazine*, 1906.

(opposite) William H. Hyde's Doveridge. Courtesy of the Cornish Historical Society.

CHAPTER 7

Doveridge: A Garden for Painters

A charming place, much more cozy than mine.[20]
—*Augustus Saint-Gaudens, 1913*

Thomas and Maria Dewing, who arrived in Cornish the year after the Saint-Gaudenses, were in part responsible for the gardening craze there. Their gardens were among the most extensive in the colony at that time, and Thomas Dewing's horticultural experimentation in finding plants that would survive in the harsh climate laid the groundwork for Stephen Parrish and other gardeners who came later. The Dewings summered in Cornish between 1886 and 1905, living in an old farmhouse they purchased from Charles C. Beaman in exchange for a portrait of Mrs. Beaman. Maria dubbed their house Doveridge after her ancestral home in England, but to the locals it was known as Low Court, because it looked straight up to High Court. (Thomas's amorous relationship with High Court's mistress, Annie Lazarus, did not go unnoticed among the colonists.)

For nearly twenty years, the Dewings were an integral part of the Cornish scene, orchestrating masques and planning elaborate dinner parties, one of Thomas's specialties. Thomas was one of the colony's most energetic personalities. "He falls right into everything like a duck into water," noted Saint-Gaudens.[21] Frances Grimes described Dewing as "the dominating person in the community. Everyone was afraid of his ridicule and in awe of his artistic

Thomas Wilmer Dewing, *The Song*, oil on canvas, 1891. Courtesy of Edward and Deborah Shein.

judgment."[22] The Dewings introduced many artists to the colony, including Frances Houston, Henry O. Walker, and Thomas's student Henry Prellwitz. His friend, artist Dennis Miller Bunker, however, could not be persuaded to join the colony. "They bore me to death with their houses and their poor little flower beds," Bunker wrote to his wife, Eleanor Hardy Bunker (who subsequently married Charles Platt after Dennis's untimely death in 1890).[23] The "poor little flower beds" at the Dewings' house would inspire other artists to create equally beautiful gardens.

Both Dewings were remarkably gifted painters who have left their mark on American art. Like many of the artists drawn to the Cornish Colony, Thomas Wilmer Dewing (1851–1938) studied in Paris before settling in New York, where he taught at the Art Students League and was a member of The Ten. He was known for his portraits (such as those of fellow Cornishites Frances Houston, Charles Platt, and Augustus Saint-Gaudens) and his ethereal land-scapes with dreamlike women who seem to float in vapor. Many of his best-known paintings, such as *Summer* (1890) and *The Song* (1891), which features Maria seated and Annie Lazarus standing, were painted in his Cornish studio.[24]

Maria Oakey Dewing (1845–1927), like many of the colony's women, had multiple talents—she was the author of *Beauty in the Household* (1882) and wrote theatricals as well as being an accomplished plein-air painter. Maria specialized in floral paintings that depict the profusion of lilies, larkspurs, poppies, and roses that grew abundantly in their garden. Not many of her paintings survive, but one of the best known was *Poppies and Italian Mignonette* (once owned by Charles Lang Freer). "I painted it at Cornish…[the] poppies grew in a large bed mixed with a tall white mignonette that grows wild in Italy.…I never saw it anywhere else than in our Cornish garden," she wrote to Freer.[25]

The Dewings' flower gardens seem to have been planted with an eye for Maria's paintings.

(top left) Thomas Dewing and his daughter Elizabeth, circa 1890. High Court can be seen in the upper right. Photo by Henry Prellwitz. Courtesy of Wendy Prellwitz.

(above) Maria Oakey Dewing, *The Garden in May*, oil on canvas, 1895. National Museum of American Art, Smithsonian Institution, Gift of John Gellatly.

(left) William H. Hyde's garden at Doveridge. Photo Jessie Tarbox Beals. Shelton, *Beautiful Gardens in America*, 1924.

Old-fashioned flowers such as dahlias, phlox, sweet william, poppies, and shrub roses are evident in her paintings. Hollyhocks lined the path that looked up to High Court, and a charming hand-crafted wooden gate (similar to the one at Crossways) and a long bench, both of Dewing's design, added the essential touches. The Dewings' plain, but comfortable outdoor porch with a brick floor was in marked contrast with High Court's elegant dining terrace. Thomas lavished as much care on his flower and vegetable gardens as he did on his paintings, but in the end the Dewings left Cornish for the quieter atmosphere of Green Hills, New Hampshire, and later Fryeburg, Maine. In 1906, Doveridge was bought by William Henry Hyde (1856-1943), who reworked the garden on a larger scale, while keeping the Dewings' original configuration and handmade gates. Later Judge Learned Hand owned the property. Today Doveridge is privately owned.

(above) Charles Platt's house and garden, with Cornish hills in background, circa 1898. Courtesy of members of the Platt family.

(opposite) The view from Platt's studio to the Cornish hills, circa 1903. Courtesy of members of the Platt family.

CHAPTER 8

Charles A. Platt's Place: An Architect's Garden

What Mr. Platt has achieved in his garden . . . is luxuriance of bloom
and foliage.
—*House and Garden*, 1924

N o one did more to mold the Cornish style of gardening than Charles Adams Platt
(1861–1933), the etcher-turned-architect who designed many of the colony's most
distinguished houses and gardens, including his own. With an artist's eye, he carefully sited each of his houses to capitalize on the individual view, but in his own place he directed the sweeping view to the green valley below and the distant hills beyond rather than
to Mount Ascutney, somewhat hidden from view by a grove of pine trees. Such a painterly
composition is not surprising; Platt was an artist at heart and an architect by profession.

Platt came to Cornish in 1889 at the invitation of Henry O. Walker, a fellow artist from
New York and one of Platt's wide circle of friends that included Saint-Gaudens, Herbert
Adams, Herbert Croly, and Stephen Parrish (with whom he had studied etching in 1880).
Platt received his art education at the National Academy of Design in New York and studied
painting in Paris. Like many of his generation, he embraced Beaux-Arts architectural philos-
ophy and particularly admired Italian Renaissance architecture, even though he was a painter
at the time. He turned his attention to landscape architecture in 1892 after traveling to Italy
with his brother William, a landscape architect and apprentice to Frederick Law Olmsted, Sr.

(the "father" of American landscape architecture). With William's encouragement, Charles's eyes were opened to Italian villas and gardens (his haunting photographs later appeared in his book, *Italian Gardens*).

Since William died shortly after their return home—Platt's first wife and newborn twins had died in 1889—Cornish and its artistic fellowship represented a new beginning for Charles Platt. He subsequently married Eleanor Bunker, Dennis Bunker's widow, who was considered one of the colony's "beauties." Platt, of course, was one of the major figures of Cornish and well respected by everyone. Laura Walker remembered him as "a quiet person and sometimes rather speechless—a man of fine feeling, a good friend and a very talented architect and landscape architect."[26]

Platt's intention as an architect was not to reproduce what he had seen in Italy, but to adapt its spirit to an American context. Cornish soon be-

came a proving ground for Platt, and within a year of his arrival he had received commissions from Henry Walker and Annie Lazarus, followed by ones from Herbert Adams, Herbert Croly, Winston Churchill, Emily Slade, and others.

Platt set the style that dominated the colony not only in his own work, but reached out to that of his protégés Ellen Shipman and, to a lesser extent, Rose Nichols. This style was a blend of Italian classicism tempered with American informality. Platt always ensured the cozy relationship of house and garden with brick terraces and indoor-outdoor areas such as a loggia or piazza to frame the view out. Following the precepts of formalism, his gardens were laid out axially, with brick paths bisecting flower beds; large Italian terra-cotta pots lined walkways and were set out at strategic points throughout the garden, as were pieces of statuary. Masses of shrubbery helped screen and control the all-important views.

(opposite) Flower gardens in 1999. Photo by David Putnam.

(below) The terrace, 1999. High Court can no longer be seen. Photo by David Putnam.

(below) The terrace at Charles Platt's place, with Sylvia Platt looking into the garden, circa 1898. High Court looms on the hillside. Courtesy of members of the Platt family.

(above) Charles Platt's painting *High Court* shows the view from his garden, circa 1892. Courtesy of members of the Platt family.

Platt's interest in plants was primarily architectural, but his association with Ellen Shipman greatly enriched his knowledge of planting design. At Faulkner Farm and The Weld (two large-scale garden commissions in Brookline, Massachusetts, that predated Platt's collaboration with Shipman), Platt's planting scheme was subservient to the dominating garden architecture. In his own country home, however, there is a relaxed quality ("home-likeness") that is lacking in his large-scale work for clients with deep pockets. Part of that intimate quality comes from the hand of Eleanor Platt, who was responsible for the garden, the selection of plants, and their color arrangements.

The year after his arrival at the colony, Platt purchased land from Chester Pike and built a studio on Plainfield Stage Road (now Platt Road). Over the next twenty or so years he expanded and refined his place, carefully considering every step of the way. Writing in 1901, Herbert Croly aptly summed up Platt's accomplishments: "The house, the garden and the grounds have all been planned so that each occupies its proper place in a general scheme, no one of the parts of which have been made especially conspicuous."[27]

Platt's low, two-story house, with its Italian-inspired pavilion (piazza) to one side, nestles into the hillside as if it were in Tuscany. The columned studio, approached from a privet-lined path that rises steeply to accommodate the terrain, lies above the house's second story. From the studio one can gaze down the central path of the flower garden

(right) Mattie Edwards Hewitt's photo of the gardens in full maturity, 1923. Courtesy of members of the Platt family.

(below) Charles Platt's studio, circa 1906. Courtesy of members of the Platt family.

out to the greater garden beyond—the distant hills. To reach the main garden, which was separated from the house by a flat green terrace, one descends onto an enclosed terrace below the house, filled with four rectangular beds subdivided with orderly walkways. Early photographs show a lush density of hardy perennials, with flowering shrubs in each of the corners. Spirea, *Rosa rugosa*, hydrangeas, and lilacs were the staples of the garden, with a seasonal parade of iris, peonies, poppies, larkspur, phlox, and asters. In 1924, *House and Garden* magazine commented, "What Mr. Platt has achieved in his gar-

den, and what every real gardener must want to achieve, is luxuriance of bloom and foliage." [28]

Happily the Platt family still occupies the house and oversees the gardens laid out a hundred years ago. While the view to the Connecticut River Valley has grown up somewhat, little else has changed. The delightful terraced gardens were restored recently and represent a collaboration between garden designer Bill Noble and the present Mrs. Platt, a gardener par excellence who personally cares for the gardens.

(left) The view to Mount Ascutney from Charles Platt's place, 1999. Photo by David Putnam.

(above) The view from the terrace at High Court, 1999. Photo by David Putnam.

(opposite) High Court, designed by Charles Platt for Annie Lazarus in 1890. Courtesy of members of the Platt family.

CHAPTER 9

High Court: An Art Patron's Garden

It is an *enchantment*. It is a Platt house in Italian villa style, with an adorable garden . . . and perhaps the greatest view of all.[29]
—*Ellen Wilson, 1913*

*I*n some ways High Court is the anomaly of the Cornish Colony. Annie Lazarus, the original owner, was neither an artist nor a writer, but a patron of the arts. She probably wasn't much of a hands-on gardener either, but her house and garden was the most high-style one in the colony. While Annie's sojourn at High Court was brief but intense, she was followed by several owners who left their personal imprints.

Annie Lazarus (1859–1945), a wealthy New Yorker and an independent-minded woman, came to Cornish in 1890 at the suggestion of her longtime friend, Thomas Dewing. Unlike the other women in the colony who nurtured spouses, children, friendships, and gardens, Annie responded to a different beat. Frances Grimes, who described Cornish as a place "where men were acknowledged to be more important than the women, where the men talked and the women listened," singled out Annie as the exception. "The one woman there who ranked as man . . . was Miss Lazarus. To me this was a new thing, to see men listening to the talk of a woman with the same kind and degree of interest they did to a man, as pleased by her praise of their work as if she had been a man and an artist." Grimes continued, "That she talked with men on subjects that men and women did not talk of together in those days shocked me."[30]

Charles Platt, *Larkspur (Garden at High Court)*, oil on canvas, 1895. Courtesy of members of the Platt family.

(left) The sweeping view to High Court in 1999. Photo by David Putnam.

(above) The hedge-lined entry drive to High Court, 1999. Photo by David Putnam.

Annie's intellectual ways and high-minded airs made her somewhat out of sync with other women in the colony. "She took long walks dressed in tailored white duck with three or four red Irish terriers racing around her," Grimes recounted. With a lorgnette in her hand, she dispensed opinions about works of art. Dewing quipped that Annie must have taken great pleasure in "looking down from her palace on the artists working in the ghetto below."[31] According to Grimes, Annie so disliked looking down at Crossways, the Houstons' house, that she "planted a line of quick-growing poplars to cut it out of her view."[32] The Houstons' luxurious house and high standards of hospitality (they served Italian food rather than the French food served at High Court) rivaled Annie's reputation as a hostess.

Soon after arriving in Cornish and buying thirty acres off Plainfield Stage Road, Annie commissioned Charles Platt to design a house high on the hilltop. Completed in 1891, it was Platt's first significant commission (his first had been a more modest house for Henry Walker in 1889). According to Keith Morgan, Platt's biographer, Platt sought the advice of Stanford White to get ideas for building a house for a client. "What I want to build is an Italian villa 3 sides of a court with a collonade [sic] in the middle. . . . Haven't you got some photo or something that would help me in regard to detail?"[33]

Platt's solution was ingenious. It was a three-sided villa, with great columns on the first story covered in grapevines and a south-facing terrace overlooking the sweep of the Connecticut River and Mount Ascutney.

Platt's long, circular entry drive, lined with Japanese hydrangeas and Lombardy poplars, wound its way up the hill, reversing itself and eventually ending in a circular courtyard at the front door. For the final approach to the house, Platt lined the drive with thick hemlock hedges to screen the view. It was not until guests walked out on the terrace that they saw the sweeping panoramic view. From the terrace, steps led down in stages to the lower ground, from which one could gaze back up at the striking villa.

So as to not interfere with the magnificent hilltop setting of the house, and the distant views afforded from it, Platt kept the landscaping solutions to a minimum. He laid out a small, walled garden adjacent to the west wing of the house. By enclosing the flower garden on all sides, it did not com-

(right) The newly refurbished sunken garden at High Court, 1999. Photo by David Putnam.

pete with the all-important vistas. The sunken garden was nearly two feet below the terrace, and while enclosed on all sides, the south-facing wall had a break in it. Frances Duncan marvelled at how one could view the mountains in the blue distance from the wide front door, while stepping from the reception room out into the garden, there was "the scent of flowers coming into the room and the color of the tall larkspurs harmonizing with the hangings on the walls." [34]

Tragedy struck in 1896 when Annie's wood-framed stucco house burned, but Platt quickly replaced it with a fire-proof brick house of similar appearance. She only enjoyed it for a few more years, because around 1900 she married an artist, John Humphreys Johnson, and moved to Italy. After becoming somewhat derelict, High Court was sold in 1902 to Norman Hapgood (1868-1937), the editor of *Collier's* and *Harper's Weekly*. Hapgood's acquaintances included Louis Shipman, who wrote for *Collier's*, and Maxfield Parrish, who would provide over sixty covers for the magazine.

Hapgood and his wife carefully brought High Court back to life again, whitewashing the bricks and painting the shutters a pale Venetian green and

the roof red. They also resurrected the walled garden, turning it into a riot of color. "Mr. Hapgood professes not to know the difference between a rose and a dandelion, but he enjoys, with the zest of a lover of Nature's beauties, the lovely wilderness of flowers which his wife has massed in her garden, a glowing spot of color on the crest of a hill." [35] Like this comment, most of the information about High Court's gardens comes from the Hapgood era. One journalist described it as "a wild tangle of blue larkspur, and in the season, purple-pink cosmos, wonderful clumps of . . . annuals of the same hue, phlox in profusion, heliotrope and other softer plants which lie close to the soil and make a rich blue carpet." [36]

As lovers of all things Italian, the Hapgoods embellished the garden with sculpture (such as a copy of Verrocchio's *Boy with a Fish*) and lavishly furnished the house with antique Italian furniture and textiles. The Hapgoods commissioned a bas-relief from Harry Thrasher (1883-1918), a local artist who subsequently died in the First World War, which is still in place today. They later sold High Court to A. Conger Goodyear, an industrialist and art collector, who called in Ellen Shipman in September 1914 to rework the garden. Shipman, who was just begin-

(left) High garden walls with an opening into the surrounding woodlands, 1999. Photo by David Putnam.

(below) The view to Mount Ascutney from the studio at High Court, 1999. Photo by David Putnam.

(bottom) Harry Thrasher's bas-relief depicting Salome dancing before Herod (1913), in garden at High Court, 1999. Photo by David Putnam.

ning to handle commissions on her own, prepared an ambitious scheme for revamping the flower beds as well as reconfiguring the garden walls into their present appearance. Shipman recommended dense clusters of perennials and annuals, rigorously maintained for perpetual bloom.

In the 1950s High Court passed to James L. Farley, a local newspaper editor who did much to keep the memory of the colony alive. He did not alter the original fabric of the garden, but instead worked to keep the all-important views open. The current owners of High Court rescued the slumbering house and garden in 1995. The sunken garden was completely overhauled and planted in a white theme, with hydrangea and rhododendron, edged with lambs ears and a thin outline of boxwood. A classic Cornish-style pool was added to the sunken garden, and other areas have been designed and planted in the spirit of both Ellen Shipman and Charles Platt. Whether it commands the finest view of Mount Ascutney is subject to debate, but it is certainly one of the most stylish gardens in the colony today.

(above) Where house and garden meet at Stephen Parrish's Northcote. *Century Magazine*, 1906.

(opposite) The gardens at Northcote, 1999. Photo by David Putnam.

CHAPTER 10

Northcote: An Amateur's Garden

> One of the most satisfying of all Cornish gardens [because] house and
> garden are inseparable.
> —*Frances Duncan, 1906*

Stephen Parrish's Northcote represents the best of Cornish gardening, from its overall conception to its skillful planting. Because of Northcote's location on an exposed hillside, where gardening was especially challenging, it is all the more remarkable. It was an amateur's garden (always the best kind), planned for its flowers rather than bound by its ingenuity. Northcote exemplifies the true mingling of house and garden in ways that other, more deliberately planned properties in the colony do not. It exudes "homelikeness" as coined by Duncan. Happily Northcote is probably the best documented garden in the colony, which played a significant role in the partial restoration by garden historian Bill Noble of Norwich, Vermont.[37] Praise was heaped on Northcote by contemporary writers such as Frances Duncan, who claimed that "no Cornish garden excelled it."[38] The artist's instinct for composition and countless hours of grueling work played equal roles in the creation of this garden.

Stephen Parrish (1846–1938), who hailed from a Philadelphia Quaker family, was a landscape painter and etcher of considerable merit, but is best remembered today as father of Maxfield Parrish. It was Charles Platt (whom he taught the art of etching) who urged him

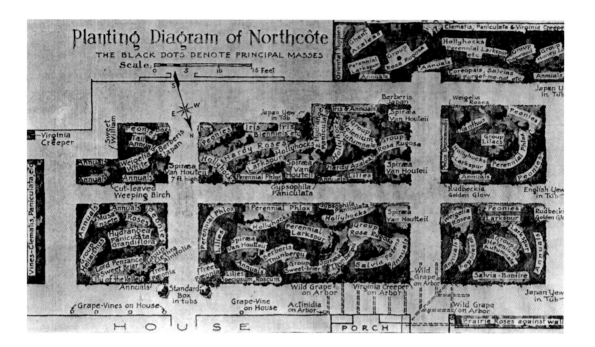

to come to Cornish in the early 1890s. In 1893 Parrish and his wife, Elizabeth Bancroft Parrish, settled on eighteen acres near the summit of a steep hillside. Unusually, Northcote faces north, without a view to Mount Ascutney. Parrish commissioned Philadelphia architect Wilson Eyre (a family friend) to design a clapboard house (subsequently painted white), and as soon as it was finished in 1894, Parrish began planting vines to cover the walls and provide a frame for his garden. These vine-covered walls enclosed the rectangular flower garden on several sides (he later built a greenhouse along the third side where he raised his annuals each year), ensuring a well-protected setting for growing vegetables, annuals, and perennials.

As his passion for garden making began to consume him (he apparently had done little gardening before moving to Cornish), Parrish began to spend most of the year at Northcote. When his wife left him in 1898 to join a religious group, Parrish was joined at Northcote by his niece Anne Parrish. Parrish's priceless garden diaries, kept between 1893 and 1910, offer solid information on how he gardened as well as glimpses of Cornish social life and family events. April 4, 1895: "Arrived at Cornish this

afternoon—a winter landscape. The season very late after the hard winter. Much snow everywhere." The next visit, May 13th, brought "cold weather following excessive heat, night *killing frost*. All my grape vines were cut down." Poignant entries reveal the extent to which his passion consumed him. November 30, 1899: "Thanksgiving. Worked in manure bin. Fred and Lydia to dinner." December 19, 1899: "Everything in ship-shape condition for the winter."[39] Frequent entries relate to the weather, ordering plants and setting them out in the garden, trimming grapevines, cleaning out the lily pools, daily battles with bugs, and all the other mundane tasks that keep a garden in top form.

Parrish's flower garden was nestled into the L of the house and laid out with axial paths. It consisted of raised beds filled at first with annuals, but by 1898 they were brimming with perennials throughout the season. Spring bulbs were followed by columbines, iris, and campanulas; these, in turn, were followed by peonies and delphiniums, including *Delphinium belladonna*. In midsummer, the garden came into its own, with hollyhocks, lilies, hardy phlox, and poppies, followed by Japanese anemones, all stalwarts of traditional New England gardens. All of Parrish's se-

(above) Northcote, designed by Philadelphia architect Wilson Eyre, 1999. Photo by David Putnam.

(left) Stephen Parrish working in his garden, Spring 1899. Dartmouth College Library.

(opposite) Stephen Parrish's planting plan for Northcote, 1902, showing a mix of winter-hardy perennials, vines, and shrubs. Courtesy of Bill Noble.

(above) Garden steps under construction, Autumn 1900. Dartmouth College Library.

(right) Stephen Parrish, *Garden Staircase*, oil on canvas, circa 1907. Private Collection.

lections were planted for rich color harmony. The enclosing walls were covered with clematis, roses, and actinidia as well as grapevines. Tubs filled with yew and box standards were positioned at regular intervals. The pièce de résistance was the seven-foot-high *Spiraea* x *vanhouttei* clipped into an arch over one of the pathways.

But Parrish was a restless gardener, and by 1905 he had widened the paths in the flower garden and removed two raised beds so he could build a sunken lily pool. Ideas evolved for developing the farther reaches of the garden where he had to deal with the windswept slope. Parrish's ingenuity is

more apparent in planning these areas than in the enclosed garden. On the outer side of the embankment, he made thick plantings of virburnum and other quick-growing shrubs. A long, low seat, designed to harmonize with the pergola, was fitted into the curve of the bank. Outside the embankment he planted young pines and created a long grass path that terminated with an old pine. He also developed a shrubbery and a pinetum (a grouping of pine trees) and built a studio and a workshop, each presenting the opportunity to create more garden pictures. His most ambitious project was The Boulevard, which kept him busy for five years.

(left) A shady bench beneath the grape arbor, with tubs of blue Otaksa hydrangeas and a mirror pool, circa 1910. Dartmouth College Library.

(below) Stephen Parrish, *Pergola at Northcote*, oil on canvas, circa 1905. Private Collection.

(right) The Boulevard in 1999. Photo by David Putnam.

Built into the hillside with masonry, it included stairs and walls. Parrish's painting *Garden Staircase* (1907) shows the low, broad steps that were totally in keeping with the more naturalistic portion of the garden.

Northcote was filled with all those "special effects" that make a garden exceptional, such as a pergola running along one side of the house to the edge of the bluff and covered with wild grapevines (*Vitis labrusca*) and Virginia creeper. The lily pool near the pergola reflected the blue Otaksa hydrangea and mirrored the clouds, creating one of the most delightful settings in all of Cornish. From the porch one could enjoy the garden's splendor, but as a hard-working gardener, Parrish probably spent more time weeding than gazing. In all, Stephen Parrish's garden at Northcote was remarkable for its intimacy, charm, and individuality, the creation of a true artist. In recent years the removal of the labor-intensive flower beds has changed the character of the garden. The refurbishment of Parrish's cherished woodland gardens and the present terrace plantings, however, makes Northcote one of the most idyllic spots in the colony.

(above) Mastlands, the home of the Dr. Arthur Nichols family, circa 1898. Photo by Rose Nichols. Courtesy of Margery P. Trumbull.

(opposite) Mrs. Arthur Nichols in the garden before the benches were added around the pool, circa 1898. Courtesy of Margery P. Trumbull.

CHAPTER 11

Mastlands: A Designer's Garden

One of the most delightful gardens . . . in garden-loving Cornish.
—*Frances Duncan, 1908*

Rose Standish Nichols (1872–1960) fell in love with Cornish in 1889, when she and her family stayed at Aspet for the summer while Uncle Gus and Aunt Gussie Saint-Gaudens were abroad. The Cornish hills were more to her liking than Rye Beach, New Hampshire, where her two younger sisters were quite content swimming, beachcombing, and playing tennis. Rose's inclination was more to the mountains than the seashore. In later years she wrote, "Few parts of New England bear so strong a resemblance to an Italian landscape as the hills rising above the banks of the Connecticut River opposite the peaks of Mount Ascutney."[40] Rose's love of the Cornish landscape sparked her career as a garden designer and writer.

Rose was the oldest of three daughters of Dr. Arthur Nichols, a homeopathic physician, and Elizabeth Homer, whose sister, Augusta, was married to Augustus Saint-Gaudens. With her younger sisters, Marian Clarke Nichols and Margaret Homer Nichols (later the wife of landscape architect Arthur Shurcliff), Rose grew up in Boston. For most of her life, she lived at 55 Mount Vernon Street, on Beacon Hill, now the Nichols House Museum. The Nichols family became permanent summer residents of the Cornish Colony in 1892.

It was at the suggestion of Uncle Gus that Rose took up the profession of garden design. She tutored privately with Charles Platt (whom she had first met in 1889) and studied independently in Boston, New York, London, and Paris. While still a fledgling designer, Rose Nichols wrote *English Pleasure Gardens* (1902), the first of three tomes devoted to historic gardens (others were on Italian and Spanish gardens), earning her a considerable reputation as a garden connoisseur. Her first book made a case for small, formal gardens that would play a pivotal role in the colony's aesthetic. A woman of many passions, in later years Rose advocated a universal love of gardens among women as a way to improve international relations. Rose is still remembered on Beacon Hill for her Sunday afternoon teas that brought together personalities in all fields for "friendly exchange of ideas in order to create a better understanding among people." [41]

The winter following the Nichols family's first summer in Cornish, Rose persuaded her father to buy the old Chester Pike farm, which included 150 acres of flatland extending from Blow-Me-Down

Brook to the Connecticut River. They renamed it Mastlands. While Dr. Nichols worked on improving the rather undistinguished 1860s farmhouse by adding a large square piazza off to one side, Rose set out to create a garden in the old farmyard enclosures. "The charming walled garden Rose designed so transformed the house that we gave up the idea of building [a new house]," her sister Margaret wrote. [42]

Rose's large walled garden (120 feet by 100 feet), separated from the piazza by a smooth grass terrace, is divided into flower beds with an orderly network of paths, the main one on axis with the piazza. The surrounding low walls are crafted from the ground's abundant stone. The rough, flat stones were laid in a rustic manner very much suited to a simple country home. Stone seats were notched into the garden walls. Rose chose an old apple tree near the center of the garden as the focal point. She designed a circular pool underneath the tree's drooping branches, surrounded by carpenter-made semicircular wooden benches painted dark green.

As with Platt, such simplicity and comfort was

(opposite) Rose Nichols in her walled garden at Mastlands. *Century Magazine*, 1906.

(left) Handcrafted stone walls with rustic seat, 1999. Photo by David Putnam.

(below) Mastlands, now the Cornish Colony Gallery and Museum, 1999. Photo by David Putnam.

(above) Circular pool and fountain, with drooping apple bough shading the semi-circular benches. *Century Magazine*, 1906.

(right) Circular pool and benches, 1999. Photo by David Putnam.

The walled gardens at Mastlands, 1999.
Photo by David Putnam.

often missing in larger, more pretentious gardens designed for clients. No wonder Rose's garden earned her high praise. Frances Duncan called it "one of the most delightful gardens in all artist-inhabited and garden-loving Cornish." [43] But what gardener is ever satisfied with their own garden? "To tell the truth," Rose wrote, "the garden as a whole verges on failure." [44] She bemoaned the fact that flowers that grew so splendidly in her neighbor's hilltop gardens would not grow in the sandy riverbed where Mastlands was located. She even had the sand dug out to a depth of three and a half feet, replacing it with rich loam, but that still did not ensure success with heavy feeders such as roses, peonies, dahlias, and Japanese iris.

After several years, Rose recognized that the garden was much too large for her and her sister to maintain properly, so she grassed over the outer flower beds. She restricted herself to phlox 'Miss Lingard', German iris, yellow daylilies, purple asters, and other hardy perennials and arranged them all for color effect. Despite the garden's problems, Rose admitted that the garden, "when seen from the safe distance of the piazza, where we live most of the summer, its deficiencies of detail are lost in space and the masses of bright-colored flowers against the gray background of stone wall, with the exquisite contours of purple Mt. Ascutney rising high above the dark pine forests in the distance, fill one with a sense of abiding peace and beauty." [45]

No other garden that Rose designed for any of her clients seems to have exuded such charm, peace, and contentment. One can only imagine the happy hours spent in this garden sheltered in the woods among dense pine trees. After years of neglect, Rose's walled garden was recently replanted with hardy New England perennials, such as asters, astilbes, campanulas, columbines, daylilies, lupine, monkshood, phlox, and poppies. While the sandy soil is still not ideal for gardening, the garden evokes the spirit of the Nichols family homestead. Mastlands is now the Cornish Colony Gallery and Museum and is open to the public during the summer months.

(above) Courtyard garden at the Hermitage, circa 1947, designed by Charles Platt in 1903 for Herbert Adams. Courtesy of Peter S. Nyboer.

(opposite) Herbert Adams, *Girl with Water Lilies*, bronze sculpture, 1928. Private Collection. Courtesy of Peter S. Nyboer.

CHAPTER 12

Hermitage: A Sculptor's Garden

Simple, but very lovely.
                                    —*May Wilkinson Mount, 1914*

Sculptor Herbert Adams (1858–1945) and his wife Adeline (Addie) Pond Adams (1859–1948) first came to Cornish in 1894, boarding at a number of farmhouses in Plainfield until 1903, when they commissioned Charles Platt to design their house and studio, known as the Hermitage. Adeline described Cornish as having "the fairest trees, hills, and skies in New Hampshire and on earth."[46] They summered in the colony until the 1940s. For a number of years, Herbert Adams was director of the Saint-Gaudens Memorial, and Adeline was a devoted member of the Mothers' and Daughters' Club and the Cornish Equal Suffrage League. Recalling her August 1913 visit to Cornish, Ellen Wilson wrote the President that the Adamses were "among the Choice spirits of the Colony—both intellectually and spiritually."[47] "Mrs. Adams charmed every one," wrote Frances Grimes.[48] She was an art critic and poet and wrote biographies of sculptors. In 1923 she published *Spirit of American Sculpture*, covering the work of Augustus Saint-Gaudens and Daniel Chester French, followed in 1932 by *Daniel Chester French, Sculptor*.

   Herbert Adams hailed from an old New England family and had studied art in Boston (against his father's wishes) and Paris before settling in New York City. Like many artists who

(opposite) Herbert Adams' studio across the courtyard, guarded by hermes (boundary gods), circa 1947. Courtesy of Peter S. Nyboer.

(right) Howard Hart's old cottage (now demolished) that was on the property, circa 1947. Courtesy of Peter S. Nyboer.

flocked to the Cornish hills, Adams shared an admiration for the art of the Italian Renaissance. Considered a protégé of Saint-Gaudens (he was also a close associate of Daniel Chester French), Adams executed bas-reliefs, sculptural fountains, portrait busts, and architectural pieces. Although he received many large civic commissions, such as the McMillan Fountain in Washington, D.C. (done in collaboration with Charles Platt) and bronze doors for the Library of Congress, he is best remembered for his portrait busts and figurative sculpture representing ideal female figures. In 1903 the Adamses bought over one hundred acres on Meriden Stage Road from Elmer Degoosh, a local farmer. The old farmhouse there was moved to another location on the property (it subsequently became Howard Hart's cottage) so that Platt's new house and studio could maximize the view to the rolling woodlands in the back and Mount Ascutney from the front door. The Hermitage also overlooks Brook Place, where the Shipman family lived from 1903 on.

Platt ingeniously connected the two-story frame house and studio with a walled courtyard so Adams could display his sculpture. A loggia, swathed in wild grapevines, ran along the front of the house and studio, and a trellis connected the two buildings along the drive. The perimeter of the formal courtyard garden was edged in low, clipped barberry (trimmed to resemble boxwood), with an urn positioned in the center of the grass terrace. A wooden gate, with one of Maxfield Parrish's brass latches, ensured their privacy. Along the studio wall, Adams placed male and female terra-cotta hermes (or boundary gods) on pedestals. "These terminal deities are the chorus in the grand opera of garden sculpture, the only rule laid upon them being that they must play the foresquare post below the waist, and look pleasant above," wrote Adeline.[49] (These terminal heads are now in a private garden in Michigan.)

Herbert Adams summed it up: "I have a place to live in, and across the lawn a place to work in, and between the two, surrounding the lawn, is my garden."[50] Adams credited his wife Adeline for doing most of the work in the garden. "We have all colors of flowers in a simple, big border of irregular form, planted with perennials and some annuals. There are peonies and larkspurs of all colors, iris, and masses of phlox with other flowers in between. . . . Peonies are set inside the barberries, with high phlox against the outer wall, and bunches of larkspur with some annuals in the middle."[51] The Adamses also had a large vegetable garden behind the studio, and in the woods Adams and his friend Howard Hart built a large amphitheater that was the scene for many amateur theatricals. Today the magical setting at the Hermitage still looks like a Willard Metcalf painting come to life.

Bacchus and Flora, terra-cotta garden
hermes at the Hermitage in winter, circa
1947. Courtesy of Peter S. Nyboer.

CHAPTER 13

Brook Place: A Landscape Architect's Garden

The perfect expression of the New England country garden.
—G. H. Edgell, 1928

The arrival of Louis Evan Shipman (1869–1933) and his wife, Ellen Biddle Shipman (1869–1950), in the 1890s represented the first of the literary folk to migrate to Cornish. They were introduced to the colony in 1894 when Marian Nichols (Rose's younger sister) invited her school friend Ellen Biddle for a visit. Ellen vividly recalled her first night in Cornish when she attended a charade party at High Court. While waiting for the fog to lift, she went out to view the terrace. She wrote:

> The valley was still filled with rolling clouds . . . in the distance was Ascutney Mountain, the Fuji-Yami of the valley, and just a few feet below, where we stood upon a terrace, was a Sunken Garden with rows bathed in moonlight of white lilies standing as an altar for Ascutney. . . . It was at that moment that a garden became for me the most essential part of a home. But years of work had to intervene before I could put this belief, born that glorious night, into actual practice.[52]

(left) Teatime under the loggia at Brook Place, 1923. Photo by Mattie Edwards Hewitt. Plainfield Historical Society.

(top) The garden front and loggia at Brook Place, remodelled by Ellen Shipman around 1907. Courtesy of Nancy Angell Streeter.

Ellen Shipman's dooryard garden at Brook Place, 1923. Clipped hemlocks mark the crossing of paths, edged with plank boards. Photo by Mattie Edwards Hewitt. Courtesy of Nancy Angell Streeter.

Born into a prominent Philadelphia family, Ellen Biddle grew up on the American frontier—Texas and the Arizona Territory—following her father, a colonel in the U.S. Army. After briefly attending school in Cambridge, Massachusetts, she married Louis Shipman, an aspiring playwright from New York who was then attending Harvard. Louis's best friend, the architectural critic Herbert Croly—who had just married Ellen's schoolmate, Louise Emory—suggested that they all share a farmhouse in Cornish. For two summers, the Shipmans and the Crolys lived at the Frank L. Johnson farmhouse (later renamed Barberry House by Homer and Carlota Saint-Gaudens).

Subsequently the Shipmans moved to Poins House, an old brick tavern in Plainfield (the name derived from one of Louis's plays), which they promptly painted white. "No one else thought of trying to live in [the house]," recalled Frances Grimes, "but the Shipmans, with their instinct for what could be made charming, saw its possibilities."[53] Little is known about their first garden, except that "fragrant flowers of our grandmother's day" lined the front walk, and at the back Ellen created a pleasant vegetable garden surrounding a stone well.[54] A low stone wall separated it from the main road. Family photographs show that everyone in the family had a hand in the garden.

While other families came to Cornish during the summer months, the Shipmans were among the few who chose to live there year-round. (Frances Grimes thought that the winter people were "more essentially Cornish.") Louis spent most of the week in New York City writing for Life and Collier's, edited by fellow Cornishite Norman Hapgood. He frequently collaborated with other writers from the colony, but one of his most famous works was his dramatization of Winston Churchill's novel, The Crises. Ellen, who was left to run the household on her own, juggled gardening and decorating with responsibilities for the couple's three children. The Shipmans, who were known for their hospitality and conviviality, were frequent guests at dinner parties and active participants in communal activities. In 1905, Ellen played Minerva (goddess of the arts and wisdom) in "A Masque of 'Ours': The Gods and the Golden Bowl," written by her husband and Percy MacKaye to honor the twentieth anniversary of the founding of the colony by the Saint-Gaudenses. Fellow tennis player Margaret Shurcliff described Louis as a "fat roly-poly author and playwright . . . dripping with perspirations [while playing] and pouring forth a continuous line of boasting and teasing."[55] Ellen, on the other hand, was a model of graciousness and aesthetic sensibilities.

Ellen's interests in gardens and architecture first surfaced when she was an adolescent, but with her move to the Cornish Colony as a newlywed she was suddenly engulfed by gardens. Routine visits to the Dewings', Stephen Parrish's, and Maxfield Parrish's fabled gardens surely inspired her latent creativity. She drew up numerous house plans for her dream house, and when Charles Platt saw some of these plans, he penned her a note that said, "If you can do as well as I saw, you better keep on."[56] To encourage her further, he made her a gift of a drawing board, a T square, and drafting equipment.

Around 1903 Ellen's wish came true when the Shipmans purchased the John Gilkey farm on Meriden Stage Road in Plainfield, renaming it Brook Place after the small mill brook running through the property. Over the course of several

(top) The Shipmans' first garden at Poins House. Ellen remodelled the window to better view the garden. *Century Magazine*, 1906.

(above) Ellen and Louis Shipman at Poins House, Plainfield, 1890s. Courtesy of Nancy Angell Streeter.

(left) Poins House in Plainfield, originally a brick tavern, 1999. Photo by Judith B. Tankard.

(right) Brick entrance terrace with buckets filled with hemlocks, 1923. Photo by Mattie Edwards Hewitt. Courtesy of Nancy Angell Streeter.

(below) Brook Place, 1999. Photo by Judith B. Tankard.

years, Ellen transformed the late-eighteenth-century farmhouse into the house and garden of her dreams. Every room in the house evoked welcome, comfort, and charm, and the gardens she created would open the door for her career.

An architectural writer singled out Ellen's achievements at Brook Place, where the garden "in its charm, seclusion, and informality, harmonizes entirely with the dwelling....[it is] a perfect expression of the New England country garden."[57] When Ellen added a new wing to the house, she designed a long brick terrace and a vine-covered rustic wood-framed loggia to create an easy transition from house to garden. Underneath the sun-filtered loggia, guests could enjoy afternoon tea while glimpsing the delicious gardens beyond. Characteristically, Ellen set the tea table on a millstone, one of several that she incorporated into her house improvements.

Like a New England dooryard garden, the main path was on axis with the door, while the cross paths were marked by four clipped hemlocks, just as Platt had done in his garden. Flower beds edged with plank boards brimmed with peonies, phlox, larkspur, and a riot of other hardy summer flowers. A tiny octagonal pool, a variation on the Cornish mirror pool, was the focal point of the long cross path. Constructed with rustic fieldstone and naturalistically planted around the edges, Shipman

reused this pool in many of her commissions. Statues were positioned at focal points against the dark green background that screened the nearby road. Simple wooden buckets (rather than terra-cotta urns) filled with clipped hemlocks were set out on either side of the main entry door. A hedge and low stone wall, with plantings of birch trees and pines, ensured privacy. Brook Place also boasted a large tennis court, laid out in an old apple orchard, where Louis Shipman spent many happy hours on weekends. Ellen also had a vegetable garden and a nursery area.

Most of what is known about Ellen Shipman's garden surfaces in Mattie Edwards Hewitt's sublime photographs, taken during the summer of 1923 (when she also photographed Aspet, Dingleton House, and the Platt place) and later published in *House and Garden*.[58] The stand of Lombardy poplars that appears in *Winter Afternoon*, Willard Metcalf's painting of Brook Place in 1917, was later replaced by hemlocks that enclose the property today. Unfortunately the hurricane of 1938 did extensive damage to some of the larger trees at Brook Place.

Ellen, who turned her talents as a gardener to profit as a professional designer around 1910 to ease the family's financial difficulties, attributed her success to working daily in her garden for fifteen years, which taught her "to know plants, their habits and

(left) The octagonal pool at Brook Place, 1999. Photo by Judith B. Tankard.

(below) Willard Metcalf, *Winter Afternoon*, oil on canvas, 1917. Courtesy of Berry-Hill Galleries, New York.

their needs."[59] Because she needed more than a knowledge of plants to be a successful garden designer, she turned to Charles Platt for tutelage in design and construction. Throughout her career, Shipman re-created the essence of the Cornish style in her nationwide commissions. A simple axial plan with luscious plantings ensured the essential close integration of house and garden. She almost always used sculptural pieces by Louis St. Gaudens, Herbert Adams, or Adams's students Willard Paddock and Edward McCartan in her commissions. Even after moving her office to New York City in the early 1920s, Shipman's ties to Cornish remained strong. Every summer she brought her office staff up on the train to Windsor, Vermont, and thence to Brook Place for work and leisure. She continued to spend summers in Cornish until she retired in 1947. Today Brook Place is owned by a young family who care for a garden filled with descendants of Shipman's plants.

CHAPTER 14

Herbert Croly's Place: A Critic's Garden

One of the most beautiful and extensive of Cornish's many lovely gardens.
—*May Wilkinson Mount, 1914*

After spending several summers in the Cornish Colony, including two with the Shipmans, Herbert D. Croly (1869–1930) and his wife, Louise, decided to buy some pastureland off the Saint-Gaudens Road and then commissioned Charles Platt to design their house. This was not a surprising choice of architect, for Croly, who later served as editor of *Architectural Record* from 1900 to 1906, had been following Platt's career closely. He championed Platt in several articles, bringing his work to greater notice. Croly was also a founding editor of the *New Republic*, and while living in Cornish, he wrote *The Promise of American Life* (1909) and *Progressive Democracy* (1914). The Crolys' impressive array of literary friends included Louis Shipman, Norman Hapgood, and Winston Churchill.

In 1897 Charles Platt designed a small L-shaped house for the Crolys on a sheltered plateau overlooking Dingleton Hill. Surrounded by rolling pastureland, the modest clapboard house has a hipped roof and a projecting loggia (piazza), with a formal garden tucked

(opposite) The Crolys' garden was divided into rectangular beds, with linear hedging enclosing it. *Century Magazine,* 1906.

(top) View down the main garden path from the piazza. Lowell, *American Gardens,* 1902.

The outline of the formal garden can be seen in Charles Platt's painting, *Garden in Winter (the Croly Garden)*, oil on canvas, circa 1904. Courtesy of members of the Platt family.

into the L of the house. In 1902 and 1904, Platt made modifications to the house. The draing room and the loggia afforded views of the flower gardens or the distant hills, depending on one's desire. In Croly's own words, "The house and garden is . . . a very good example of what can be done at a comparatively small expense in the way of building up a complete country place."[60] The aesthetic of this delightful country place was strikingly different than that of High Court, designed seven years earlier, or Platt's own house.

By present-day standards, the garden was complex and maintenance-intensive, far more formal than the house. Laid out on a rectangular grid, with the main axial path leading out from the living room door, Platt divided it into a four-square lower garden and a slightly elevated upper garden of two beds. The layout can be seen in Platt's painting, Garden in Winter. Typical of many of the gardens in Cornish, it hugs the house and serves as outdoor living space. It is enclosed on two sides by the house and lattice that screens the kitchen yard; white-painted wooden walls frame the rest of the garden. None of the ornament so prevalent in Cornish gardens is here, the flowers and the planting artistry being the chief ornamental features.

Like any well-designed garden, the secret of the Croly garden lies in its variety of foliage. The latticework screening the kitchen yard was copiously covered in clematis, with lilacs, barberry, and other hardy shrubs growing at the foot. Clematis, bittersweet, and actinidia cover the long white wall, with a bed of showy hollyhocks underneath. The distinctive foliage of wild grapevines covering the piazza frames the view out to the lower garden, and what a garden! Here is Croly's own description of it: "The narrow bed to the right is planted with a row of Spirea Thunbergii in front and with forsythia and Japanese honeysuckle behind. The low hedge, which outlines the two beds to the left, is composed of Japanese barberry."

Another hedge of Spiraea x vanhouttei helps provide shelter for the enclosure. The main path is lined with peonies, with masses of larkspur behind; in the autumn, hardy asters come into bloom. The beds in the upper garden are larger (14' x 25'), "requiring great masses of foliage and flowers to fill them," in this case hydrangeas, annuals, and roses. In the distance, a large elm tree and stands of pine trees frame the garden.

Croly mused that his house and garden were pleasant to live in, but the maintenance required "persistent attention and hard, but remunerative work."[61] Herbert Croly and his wife, Louise, lie next to another great gardener, Ellen Shipman, in the Gilkey Cemetery on Stage Road behind Brook Place.

Herbert Croly's house and garden,
designed by Charles Platt in 1897.
Lowell, *American Gardens*, 1902.

(above) The dreamy entrance to The Oaks, Maxfield and Lydia Parrish's home in Plainfield, circa 1905. Alma Gilbert Collection.

(opposite) Ancient oaks at The Oaks, 1999. Photo by David Putnam.

The Oaks: A Dream Garden

> Artists of Cornish consider the Maxfield Parrish gardens very wonderful and very exquisite.[62]
> —*May Wilkinson Mount, 1914*

Maxfield Parrish represented the first of a younger generation of artists who found the peaceful atmosphere of the Cornish Colony beckoning them. Thanks to his success as an illustrator, he was able to invest in a piece of the colony in 1898 when he bought nineteen acres of rocky pasture from a local farmer. No doubt what drew Parrish to the site on Freeman Hill in Plainfield was its stand of ancient white oaks and the sweeping view across the Connecticut River Valley. Edith Wharton gasped at "the divine view of Mount Ascutney" when she and Teddy paid a visit in August 1905, declaring it "the most beautiful I have ever seen in America." [63] This was high praise indeed from one of America's leading literary lights known for her discerning judgment. Parrish's house and its garden would prove to be one of the most individual in the colony and entirely different from his father's at Northcote.

The son of Stephen and Elizabeth Parrish, Frederick Maxfield Parrish (1870–1966) was born into the distinguished Philadelphia Quaker family. Like his father, Fred (as he was known to intimates) leaned to the art world (rather than the medical world of his ancestors), attending Haverford College and the Pennsylvania Academy of the Fine Arts. After his marriage in

The divine view of Mount Ascutney, 1999. Photo by David Putnam.

1895 to Lydia Austin (1872–1953), an art instructor at the Drexel Institute, he began illustrating children's books, such as L. Frank Baum's *Mother Goose in Prose*, and dreaming of moving from Philadelphia to Cornish, a better working environment. His subsequent career as America's most beloved artist is legend, but his charming house and garden at The Oaks still remains a well-kept secret.

When Maxfield bought (with money borrowed from his father) the unpromising rough sheep pasture on Freeman Hill, he must have envisioned a comfortable, unpretentious house that would sit well among the surrounding oaks and pines (*Pinus strobus*). Dubbing it The Oaks, he deferred to the magnificent trees that still grace the site today. With an artist's vision, he planned the house and garden to maximize the view out. Unlike most of the architect-designed houses that made the colony famous, such as those by Charles Platt and Wilson Eyre (who had designed his father's house), The Oaks was designed by the owner himself, who had an instinctive perception of architectural design. Herbert Croly deemed The Oaks "one of the few American houses possessing genuine architectural character…it is very personal, it is very local, it is very American." [64] Croly even suggested that Parrish might have made a good architect had he not been a painter. Homer Saint-Gaudens took it

one step further, saying The Oaks was a "child's dream house in every sense of the word." [65]

Parrish planned the long, low house to gracefully stretch from east to west along the rocky ridge of a steep hill. His masterful siting of the house among the oaks gave new meaning to the colony's tradition of houses that were inseparable from the landscape. There were no architectural plans for The Oaks; it just evolved. Over the years, as his career swelled and the number of his children increased, Parrish made many improvements at The Oaks, including building a separate studio up the hill to ensure a better (and more private) work place. The studio was equipped with a machine shop where he designed latches and hinges (they were cast for him at Ascutney Forge) found in many Cornish gardens.

Parrish's diversity as an artist—he was a mechanic, stonemason, carpenter, cabinetmaker, metalsmith, and photographer—played a role in planning the garden. After a three-month sojourn in Italy in 1903 to illustrate the Wharton book, *Italian Villas and Their Gardens*, Parrish's gardens (and artwork) began to take on a diluted classical appearance. "The garden is a delightful tangle [with] a few magnificent trees and a really stupendous view…altogether it is an ideal artist home," Ellen Wilson wrote in a letter to the President dated 1913. [66] The garden was only

(above) The long, low house stretches east to west, with walled garden below, and studio just visible behind the house. Alma Gilbert Collection.

(left) A dream garden in midsummer at The Oaks, circa 1915. Alma Gilbert Collection.

(left) Terrace gardens at The Oaks, 1999. Photo by David Putnam.

(below) Lydia Parrish admiring a fine stand of hollyhocks, circa 1912. Alma Gilbert Collection.

(opposite) Maxfield Parrish's oil painting, *A Shower of Fragrance*, cover for *Ladies Home Journal*, July 1912, shows cascades of spirea. Private Collection. Photo Alma Gilbert Collection.

barely beginning to take shape at the time of Frances Duncan's article in 1905. When her editor enquired why there were no photographs of the garden, Parrish responded that he was only beginning to make a garden. "There is nothing but raw dirt hauled here and there, but some day, some day, we are going to have an affair which will make Versailles look like a dory full of portulacas," he wrote.[67]

One of the most celebrated components of the Parrish garden was the loggia running along one side of the house. Covered in grapevines, the loggia provided an outdoor living space from which to gaze at the view beyond while looking at the garden in the foreground. From the loggia, steps led down to the terrace below the house that further framed the expansive view. Enclosed by low, stone retaining walls, the 50' x 34' grass terrace was planned as a good place to step back and admire the

house. Urns carefully placed atop stone piers of the garden walls looked just like, well, a Parrish painting. In the center of the terrace, a large reflecting pool sixteen feet in diameter mirrored the heavens and the oak trees.

One decidedly quirky element in Parrish's scheme is the massive stone gate leading from the edge of the pasture to the garden—its commanding size seems a fitting entry for a king and queen. Parrish's own photographs show how the shadows of the oak leaves dappled the arch and wall of stone and weather-beaten plaster. The flower borders along the stone walls were filled with a riot of perennials, such as iris, lupine, peonies, phlox, and other Cornish favorites. Masses of towering hollyhocks bloomed along the front of the house, and a broad grass path was bordered by the clouds of *Spiraea* x *vanhouttei* that pervades his artwork. Lilacs and apple blossoms completed the picture, in all, an

THE LADIES' HOME JOURNAL

JULY 1912

PAINTED BY MAXFIELD PARRISH

THE CURTIS PUBLISHING COMPANY PHILADELPHIA

15 CENTS

(right) The massive gate, a fitting entry for a king and queen, 1999. Photo by David Putnam.

(bottom) Urn and *Spiraea* x *vanhouttei* at The Oaks. Photo by Maxfield Parrish, circa 1920. Dartmouth College Library.

(opposite) A sixteen-foot-wide circular pool mirrors the gardens, circa 1920. Alma Gilbert Collection.

artist's conception of a garden. In 1914, May Mount provided a delicious description of the gardens at The Oaks:

> *Designed and planted by the artist, years have been spent in adorning successive terraces with low stone walls, overhung with opulent vines, and inclosing [sic] masses of blooming flowers and contrasting shrubbery. Here, as in many another Cornish garden, one finds bright masses of tall phlox, which attain great perfection in the kindly atmosphere of this place.*[68]

The beautiful landscape at The Oaks lives on in many of Parrish's famous artworks. Not only was The Oaks a family home for Lydia and Maxfield and their four children, it was also the setting for delightful pastimes when they entertained guests—in par-

ticular Maxfield loved playing charades. The large oak-paneled music room (added in 1906) had a stage at one end, the scene of many entertainments. "The Maxfield Parrish menage is *charming* in every respect," wrote Ellen Wilson. "In the first place they are all so good-looking! He is really a beautiful young man and charming, too, and she is *lovely*, with deep dark eyes, and a sweet, rather worn look like a young madonna."[69] Lydia was a member of the Equal Suffrage League and the Mothers' and Daughters' Club in Plainfield, and in later years wrote a book *Slave Songs of the Georgia Sea Islands* (1935). Today a somewhat forgotten figure alongside her husband's towering presence, Lydia played an important role in the gardens at The Oaks. Maxfield Parrish's final years were spent painting landscapes, many fanciful versions of the local scenery.

(above) Winston Churchill standing in garden at Harlakenden House. Photo by Mary Northend. Courtesy of the Society for the Preservation of New England Antiquities, Boston.

(opposite) The view to Mount Ascutney from Harlakenden House, circa 1913–15. Dartmouth College Library.

CHAPTER 16

Harlakenden House: A Writer's Garden

One can gaze upon the most beautiful landscape to be seen from Cornish.
—May Wilkinson Mount, 1914

Harlakenden House owes its fame to several circumstances. It was one of Charles Platt's grandest commissions, and it was the home of the celebrated novelist Winston Churchill, who took pains not to be confused with the other Winston Churchill. (Sir Winston graciously added Spencer to his name to avoid confusion.) Harlakenden also served as the Summer White House in 1913–1915 for newly elected President Woodrow Wilson.

The Cornish Winston Churchill (1871–1947) hailed from St. Louis, Missouri, and was a graduate of the United States Naval Academy in Annapolis. He began his career editing the *Army and Navy Journal*, but soon found a niche for himself writing novels, such as *Richard Carvel* (1899), which responded to America's taste for fast-paced historical fiction. In a few short years, his best-sellers earned him the accolade of "the most popular author of fiction in America between 1900 and 1925" and also made him wealthy.[70] His literary earnings provided Churchill with the means to enjoy life to its fullest.

(right) Harlakenden House, an elegant Georgian-style house designed by Charles Platt for Winston Churchill and Mabel Harlakenden Churchill in 1899. It served as the Summer White House 1913–15. Dartmouth College Library.

(below) The octagonal pool and benches in the courtyard garden, circa 1913-15. Dartmouth College Library.

Churchill came to the Cornish Colony in 1898 at the suggestion of fellow writer Louis Shipman (who, unfortunately, never became as financially successful). Armed with money and ambition, Churchill commissioned Charles Platt to design a Georgian-style house in 1899. The expansive house (which burned in 1923) was sited on a bluff overlooking the Connecticut River. Churchill named it Harlakenden House, after his wife Mabel Harlakenden Hall. The Churchills numbered many of the colonists, especially Maxfield and Stephen Parrish, among their friends. Mabel Churchill, who was known for her beauty, occasionally modeled for Maxfield. Over the next decade or so, Winston continued to acquire land, mostly forested area that he managed. As his land acquisitions expanded, he became increasingly involved in politics, serving in the New Hampshire legislature. He was also among the first to acquire an automobile in Cornish.

Harlakenden House was the largest residence that Platt designed in the area. According to Keith Morgan, it was unusual because it was not a simple artist's retreat, like many of the other houses in the colony, but a full-blown country house.[71] The scale of the house and its opulent furnishings—including tapestries hanging on the walls, satin furniture, and portraits of great Americans—seemed an anomaly in the colony. Churchill was trying to evoke a Maryland country estate with all the trappings, and part of the trappings included a 500-acre woodland park that abutted the house. "Winston Churchill, himself, laid out gardens and park in an Old English style, planned roadways and drives, and thinned the woods. . . . Vistas and views have been opened up, showing the wide sweep of the valley here, the crest of mountains there, and clustering vines and shrubbery about some picturesque nook."[72]

(left) Ellen Axson Wilson, *The Terrace*, oil on canvas, 1913. Private Collection. The identity of this garden is uncertain, but it probably is Harlakenden.

(below) The garden at Windfield, 1997. Photo by Judith B. Tankard.

The formal gardens took the form of a central courtyard between the house and flanking wings and a terrace garden adjacent to the gallery. Grapevines covered the small latticework pavilion in the center of one wall, where a photograph shows Winston standing with a book in hand. An octagonal pool and benches in the walled garden provided a secluded setting. From the back of the house, Winston could "gaze upon the most beautiful landscape to be seen in Cornish."[73]

Because Harlakenden was both secluded and commodious, and the Churchills were gracious hosts, it was a natural choice for Woodrow Wilson's Summer White House. In 1913, in honor of newly elected President Wilson's visit, Dr. Arthur Nichols planted a long avenue of pine trees, starting at Chaseholm (just down the road from Mastlands) to the entrance of Harlakenden.[74] First Lady Ellen Axson Wilson (1860–1914), an amateur artist who had studied at the Art Students League of New York with both Brush and Dewing and who had been affiliated with the artists' colony in Old Lyme (Connecticut), spent the summer of 1913 in Cornish at her doctor's advice (she died the next summer). Her frequent letters to her husband about social events that she squeezed in between painting depict a vivid picture of colony life. Luncheons, teas, and dances seemed to fill the days. The Wilsons enjoyed the lively company of their Cornish neighbors, dining frequently with Stephen, Maxfield, and Lydia Parrish. Returning to Washington after one visit, President Wilson wrote his wife: "How shall I tell you what those eight days at Cornish meant to me! They were like a new honeymoon! All the days were days of contentment, renewal, and delight."[75]

The Churchills moved to Windfield House on Freeman Road, Plainfield, after Harlakenden burned in 1923. Winston outfitted the house with furnishings saved from Harlakenden and paneled the living and dining rooms himself. Giving up writing for a number of years, Churchill devoted himself to painting during his final years. A small, but attractive Cornish-style garden is part of the property today. In 1928 a new house was erected on the site of Harlakenden House, roughly covering the area of the servant's wing. Peabody and Stearns architects also laid out an attractive English-style sunken garden, with a stone pergola and a garden house, currently under restoration.

(above) Dingleton House Gardens, 1999.
Photo by David Putnam.

(opposite) Dingleton House, circa 1930s.
Courtesy of Grace Bulkeley.

CHAPTER 17

Dingleton House: An Italian Garden

> Unquestionably the most beautiful and complete pleasure grounds in Cornish to-day.[76]
> —*Rose Standish Nichols, 1924*

Dingleton House, Platt's last house and garden project in the colony, was the most elaborate and perhaps the most skillfully designed of all. His clients were Emily Slade, a sculptor and amateur woodworker from New York, and her sister, Augusta. The Slades purchased over a hundred acres on Dingleton Hill in 1903 and the next year commissioned Platt to design their house.

Located on the side of a steep hill (especially treacherous in the winter), Dingleton House commands an excellent view of Mount Ascutney. Unlike many of his other Cornish houses, Platt sited the low, two-story house practically in the woods. While the form of the house is somewhat reminiscent of his earlier ones, Platt was able to spare no expense in building this one. In addition to large, generous rooms, the house is further distinguished by woodcarvings in the entrance hall that were designed and executed by Emily Slade, modeled after French Renaissance woodwork.

A long colonnaded loggia extending along the south side of the house affords a comfortable position for enjoying the incomparable view. Like High Court, the formal gardens were located so as not to conflict with the view. Herbert Croly remarked in 1907, three years after

(right) Dingleton House, 1999. Photo by David Putnam.

the house was built, that "when this garden is fully grown, it will be one of the most beautiful in the country; and its beauty will consist precisely of the admirable manner in which it has fitted to the plan of the house, and to the layout and the planting of the surrounding land."[77]

Unlike the dooryard gardens that inspired many of the colony's gardens, Dingleton House is a formal Italian garden in overall concept and in its architectural furnishings. In some respects the layout bears a strong resemblance to Platt's larger commissions outside the colony. The beauty of the gardens at Dingleton House lies in their strong axial layout, attractive latticework and ornamental detail, and layers of views to the immediate surrounding woodlands and to distant Mount Ascutney. The Slades and not the architect conceived the planting designs that so distinguished the gardens.

The large garden enclosure, entered through a gate in the entry court, is divided into three distinct areas connected by a long axial path. The main flower garden, adjacent to the library and studio, are bounded by low walls, with Italian planters arranged along the top. The low terrace walls frame the view to the surrounding woodlands and to Mount Ascutney in the distance. Four rectangular flower beds surround a circular pool with a fountain; four outer beds are copiously planted with hardy phlox, iris, gladioli, dwarf *Rosa wichuraiana*, and various annuals and edged with Japanese barberry. Architectural elements, including a wall fountain and antique marble sarcophagus, large tubs filled with clipped trees, and small planters lining the edge of the pool, provide the decorative touches.

An attractive pergola with latticework walls encloses the north side of the garden and separates it from the woodland. Designed by Emily Slade, the long flower borders flanking the path leading to the rose garden were edged with sweet alyssum and filled with hardy plants, such as daylilies, phlox, and larkspur. The rose garden, on slightly elevated ground and circular in shape, is delineated by a hemlock hedge, with borders of phlox, iris, peonies, and annuals that fill in for the roses when they are not in bloom. Rose Nichols identifies the roses as 'Killarney' (pale pink), 'Radiance', 'Frau Karl Druschki', and 'Gruss an Teplitz' (crimson). The four flower beds converge on a central pool edged with alyssum. A semicircular niche furnished with a wooden bench, an arbor covered with climbing roses, and a statue of Pan complete the picture.

The picture-book quality of the gardens can be attributed to Platt's architectural structuring and to

(left) The circular rose garden, sheltered by high hemlock hedges. Photo by Mattie Edwards Hewitt. Shelton, *Beautiful Gardens in America*, 1924.

(below) Rose garden through the arch at Dingleton House, 1999. Photo by David Putnam.

the seven gardeners whom the Slade sisters are reputed to have retained. The elaborate formal gardens "were tended by Scottish gardeners who thought nothing of turning hemlocks into peacocks, to the consternation of the natives."[78]

The present owner, whose family has been at Dingleton House since 1936, has managed beautifully on far fewer gardeners, namely herself, and the gardens today bear her imprint. While the density of the plantings has been reduced somewhat, their quality has become more personal, even romantic. The wonderful Platt structure allows the owner to do as she likes. "I don't think of myself as a gardener, but I can't imagine living without a garden."[79] The gardens at Dingleton House are probably the most romantic in the colony today and certainly live up to Croly's prediction that they are one of the most beautiful in the country. Part of their charm is that the whole family tends them. Good bones, good plantings, and a beautiful location are hard to beat.

(above) Pergola and pool at Dingleton House, 1999. Photo by David Putnam.

Resources

Chesterwood
National Trust for Historic Preservation
4 Williamsville Road (P.O. Box 827)
Stockbridge, Massachusetts 01262
413-298-3579
Open May through October

Cornish Colony Gallery and Museum
RR3 Box 292 Route 12-A
Cornish New Hampshire 03745
603-675-6000
Open June through October

Cornish Historical Society
RR 2 Box 416
Cornish, New Hampshire 03745

Historic Windsor, Inc.
P.O. Box 1777
Windsor, Vermont 05089-0021
802-674-6752
Sponsors garden tours
www. historicwindsor.com

Nichols House Museum
55 Mount Vernon Street
Boston, Massachusetts 02108
617-227-6993
Open all year except January

Plainfield Historical Society
P.O. Box 107
Plainfield, New Hampshire 03781

Saint-Gaudens National Historic Site
National Park Service
RR3 Box 73
Cornish, New Hampshire 03745
603-675-2175
Open late May through October
www.sgnhs.org

Woodrow Wilson House
National Trust for Historic Preservation
2340 S. Street N.W.
Washington, D.C. 20008
202-387-4062
www.nationaltrust.org

Notes

Introduction

1. Edith Bolling (Galt) Wilson, *My Memoir* (New York, 1938), 69-74, cited in Hugh Mason Wade, *A Brief History of Cornish 1763-1974* (Hanover, N.H.: University Press of New England, 1976), 77.
2. Helen W. Henderson, "An Impression of Cornish," *The Lamp* 27 (October 1903): 185.
3. Rose Standish Nichols, "A Hilltop Garden in New Hampshire," *House Beautiful*, March 1924, 237.

Chapter 1

1. Daniel Chester French, letter to Augustus Saint-Gaudens, July 8, 1887. Special Collections, Dartmouth College Library.

Chapter 2

2. Laura M. Walker, *Memories* (privately printed, 1938), courtesy of Jacqueline Walker Smith.
3. Frances Grimes, "Reminiscences," cited in Susan Faxon Olney, John Dryfhout et al., *A Circle of Friends: Art Colonies of Cornish and Dublin* (Durham, N.H.: University Art Galleries, 1985), 61.
4. Ibid., 63.
5. Ibid.
6. Margaret Shurcliff, *Lively Days: Some Memoirs of Margaret Homer Shurcliff* (Taipei: Literature House, 1965).
7. Walker, *Memories*.

8. Lydia Parrish, "Diaries," July 28, 1906, Dartmouth College Library.
9. William Pear, Nichols House Museum, Boston, Mass., interview with Alma Gilbert, October, 1998.

Chapter 3

10. Maxfield Parrish, Jr., letter to his brother Dillwyn Parrish, July 4, 1949, Alma Gilbert Papers, Dartmouth College Library.
11. Ibid., July 29, 1949.

Chapter 4

12. Augustus Saint-Gaudens, letter to Maxfield Parrish, 1901, Dartmouth College Library.
13. Maxfield Parrish, letter to Augustus Saint-Gaudens, 1906, Dartmouth College Library.
14. Edward Bok, *The Americanization of Edward Bok* (New York: Charles Scribner's Sons, 1923).

Chapter 5

1. Ellen Shipman, "Garden Note Book," circa 1947, 2, Rare and Manuscripts Collection, Cornell University Library.
2. Letters of Ellen Axson Wilson, cited in Virginia Reed Colby and James B. Atkinson, *Footprints of the Past* (Concord, N.H.: New Hampshire Historical Society), 430, 433, 435.
3. Frances Duncan, "The Gardens of Cornish," *Century Magazine* 72 (May 1906): 4.

4. Ibid., 18.

5. "Maxfield Parrish's Home and How He Built It," *The Country Calendar*, September 1905, 435-37; "An Artist's New Hampshire Garden," *Country Life in America*, March 1907, 516-20; "A Cornish Garden," *Country Life in America*, March 1908, 507-8. For many years she rented Cherry Hill Farm on Dingleton Hill, but she eventually left Cornish and moved to California. For more on Frances Duncan, see Virginia Lopez Begg, "Frances Duncan: The 'New Woman'," *Journal of the New England Garden History Society* 2 (1992): 29-35.

6. Duncan, "Gardens of Cornish," 18.

7. Mary Caroline Crawford, "Homes and Gardens of Cornish," *House Beautiful*, April 1906, 14.

8. May Wilkinson Mount, "The Gardens of Cornish," *Suburban Life*, March 1914, 133.

9. Frances Duncan, "How To Make an Old-Fashioned Garden," *Ladies' Home Journal*, April 1909, 56.

10. Shipman, "Garden Note Book," 2.

11. Mount, "The Gardens of Cornish," 136.

12. Mrs. Daniel Chester French, *Memories of a Sculptor's Wife* (Boston: Houghton Mifflin, 1928), 182.

13. Frances Grimes, "Reminiscences," cited in Susan Faxon Olney, John Dryfhout, et al., *A Circle of Friends: Art Colonies of Cornish and Dublin* (Durham, N.H.: University Art Galleries, 1985), 61.

14. Mount, "The Gardens of Cornish," 135.

Chapter 6

15. Homer Saint-Gaudens, ed., *The Reminiscences of Augustus Saint-Gaudens*, vol. 1 (New York: Century, 1913), 316.

16. Margaret Shurcliff, *Lively Days: Some Memoirs of Margaret Nichols Shurcliff* (Taipei: Literature House, 1965), 87-88.

17. Hugh Mason Wade, *A Brief History of Cornish 1763-1974* (Hanover, N.H.: University Press of New England, 1976), 50.

18. Richardson Wright, ed., "In a Sculptor's Garden: The Augustus Saint Gaudens Estate in Cornish, N.H.," *House and Garden Second Book of Gardens* (New York: Condé Nast, 1927), 22-23.

19. Ellen Shipman, "The Saint-Gaudens Memorial Gardens," *Bulletin of the Garden Club of America*, May 1948, 64.

Chapter 7

20. *Reminiscences of Augustus Saint-Gaudens*, vol. 1, 323.

21. Ibid., 323.

22. Grimes, "Reminiscences," cited in *A Circle of Friends*, 64.

23. Cited in Susan Hobbs, "Thomas Dewing in Cornish, 1885-1905," *The American Art Journal* 17 (Spring 1985): 4, note 11.

24. For more on Thomas Dewing's career, see Susan A. Hobbs, *The Art of Thomas Wilmer Dewing: Beauty Reconfigured* (Washington, D.C.: Smithsonian Institution Press/The Brooklyn Museum, 1996).

25. Jennifer Martin, "Portraits of Flowers: The Out-of-Doors Still-Life Paintings of Maria Oakey Dewing," *American Art Review* 4 (December 1977): 118.

Chapter 8

26. Laura M. Walker, *Memories* (privately printed, 1938).

27. Herbert D. Croly, "The House and Garden of Mr. Charles A. Platt," *House and Garden*, December 1901, 17.

28. "The New Hampshire Garden of Charles A. Platt," *House and Garden*, April 1924, 66-67.

Chapter 9

29. Ellen Wilson, letter to President Wilson, August 4, 1913, cited in Colby and Atkinson, *Footprints*, 432.

30. Grimes, "Reminiscences," cited in *A Circle of Friends*, 64.

31. Wade, *A Brief History of Cornish*, 54.

32. Grimes, "Reminiscences," cited in *A Circle of Friends*, 69.

33. Keith N. Morgan, "Charles A. Platt's Houses and Gardens in Cornish, New Hampshire," *The Magazine Antiques*, July 1982, 120.

34. Duncan, "The Gardens of Cornish," 10.

35. Mount, "The Gardens of Cornish," 136.

36. Helen W. Henderson, "High Court," *House and Garden*, July 1905, 22.

Chapter 10

37. See William Noble, "Northcote: An Artist's New Hampshire Garden," *Journal of the New England Garden History Society* 2 (Fall 1992): 1-9.

38. Duncan, "The Gardens of Cornish," 16; Duncan, "An Artist's New Hampshire Garden," 517.

39. Northcote Record Book, Box 3, Folder 45, Stephen Parrish Papers, Special Collections, Dartmouth College Library.

Chapter 11

40. Nichols, "A Hilltop Garden in New Hampshire," 237.

41. George Taloumis, "Rose Standish Nichols: Sixty Years Ago She Organized the Beacon Hill Reading Club (1896)," *Boston Sunday Globe*, September 16, 1956.

42. *Lively Days*, 34.

43. Duncan, "A Cornish Garden," 507.

44. Rose Standish Nichols, "How Not To Make a Flower Garden," *House Beautiful*, September 1911, 103.

45. Ibid., 104.

Chapter 12

46. "An Artist Colony, " *New York Sunday Tribune*, August 11, 1907, cited in Sylvia Yount, *Maxfield Parrish, 1870-1966* (New York: Harry N. Abrams, Inc./Pennsylvania Academy of the Fine Arts, 1999), 70.

47. Cited in Colby and Atkinson, *Footprints*, 122.

48. Cited in Olney, et al., *A Circle of Friends*, 63.

49. Adeline Adams, *The Spirit of American Sculpture* (New York: National Sculpture Society, 1923), 172.

50. Mount, "The Gardens of Cornish," 135.

51. Ibid., 136.

Chapter 13

52. Shipman, "Garden Note Book," 1.

53. Frances Grimes, "Reminiscences," undated typescript, Special Collections, Dartmouth College Library.

54. Crawford, "Homes and Gardens of Cornish," 14.

55. *Lively Days,* 35.

56. Shipman, "Garden Note Book," 3.

57. G.H. Edgell, *American Architecture of To-Day* (New York: Charles Scribner's Sons, 1928), 125.

58. "A New Hampshire House and Garden: Brook Place at Cornish, N.H.," *House and Garden*, March 1924, 75-77.

59. Shipman, "Garden Note Book," 4.

Chapter 14

60. H.D. C[roly], "A Small New Hampshire Garden," *House and Garden*, May 1902, 204.

61. Ibid., 201-4.

Chapter 15

62. Mount, "The Gardens of Cornish," 136.

63. Eleanor Dwight, *Edith Wharton: An Extraordinary Life* (New York: Harry N. Abrams, 1994), 123.

64. [Herbert Croly], "The House of Mr. Maxfield Parrish," *Architectural Record*, September 1907, 273.

65. Cited in Yount, *Maxfield Parrish, 1870-1966*, 50.

66. Colby and Atkinson, *Footprints*, 430.

67. Maxfield Parrish, letter to Richard W. Gilder, January 22, 1906, the Century Collection, New York Public Library, cited in Olney et al., *A Circle of Friends*, 48.

68. Mount, "The Gardens of Cornish, 133-35.

69. Cited in Colby and Atkinson, *Footprints*, 430.

Chapter 16

70. Ibid., 156.

71. Morgan, "Charles A. Platt's Houses and Gardens in Cornish, New Hampshire," 125.

72. Mount, "The Gardens of Cornish," 135-36.

73. Ibid., 136.

74. Wade, *A Brief History of Cornish*, 75.

75. Cited in Atkinson and Colby, *Footprints*, 425.

Chapter 17

76. Nichols, "A Hilltop Garden in New Hampshire," 238.

77. Herbert Croly, "A Cornish House and Garden," *Architectural Record* 22 (September 1907): 297,

78. Wade, *A Brief History of Cornish*, 83.

79. Grace Bulkeley, cited in Patricia Thorpe, "Down the Garden Path," *House and Garden*, July 1988, 154.

Bibliography

Selected Books and Exhibition Catalogs

Adams, Adeline. *Daniel Chester French, Sculptor.* Boston: Houghton Mifflin, 1932.

Adams, Adeline. *The Spirit of American Sculpture.* New York: National Sculpture Society, 1923.

Aucella, Frank J.; Hobbs, Patricia A.; Saunders, Frances W. *Ellen Axson Wilson First Lady—Artist.* Washington, D.C., Woodrow Wilson House, 1993.

The American Renaissance, 1876-1917. New York: Pantheon Books/Brooklyn Museum, 1979.

Blanchan, Neltje. *The American Flower Garden.* New York: Doubleday, Page, 1909.

Child, William H. *A History of the Town of Cornish, New Hampshire, 1763-1910.* Concord, N.H.: Rumford Press, 1910.

Colby, Virginia Reed, and Atkinson, James B. *Footprints of the Past: Images of Cornish, New Hampshire and the Cornish Colony.* Concord, N.H.: New Hampshire Historical Society, 1996.

Cresson, Margaret French. *Journey into Fame.* Cambridge, Mass.: Harvard University Press, 1947.

Dryfhout, John H. *The Work of Augustus Saint-Gaudens.* Hanover, N.H.: University Press of New England, 1982.

French, Mrs. Daniel Chester. *Memories of a Sculptor's Wife.* Boston: Houghton Mifflin, 1928.

Gerdts, William H. *Down Garden Paths: The Floral Environment in American Art.* Cranbury, N.J.: Associated University Presses, 1983.

Gilbert, Alma. *Maxfield Parrish: The Landscapes.* Berkeley: Ten Speed Press, 1998.

Griswold, Mac and Eleanor Weller. *The Golden Age of American Gardens: Proud Owners, Private Estates, 1890-1940.* New York: Harry N. Abrams, 1991.

Hill, May Brawley. *Grandmother's Garden: The Old-Fashioned American Garden, 1865-1915.* New York: Harry N. Abrams, 1995.

Hobbs, Susan A. *The Art of Thomas Wilmer Dewing: Beauty Reconfigured.* New York: Smithsonian Institution/Brooklyn Museum, 1995.

Leighton, Ann. *American Gardens of the Nineteenth Century: For Comfort and Affluence.* Amherst: University of Massachusetts Press, 1987.

Lowell, Guy, ed. *American Gardens.* Boston: Bates and Guild, 1902.

MacAdam, Barbara J. *Winter's Promise: Willard Metcalf in Cornish, New Hampshire, 1909-1920.* Hanover, N.H.: Hood Museum of Art, 1998.

Monograph on the Work of Charles A. Platt. Introduction by Royal Cortissoz. New York: Architectural Book Publishing, 1913.

Morgan, Keith N. *Charles A. Platt: The Artist as Architect.* Cambridge, Mass.: The MIT Press, 1985.

Morgan, Keith N. *Shaping an American Landscape: The Art and Architecture of Charles A. Platt.* Hanover, N.H.: University Press of New England/Hood Museum of Art, 1995.

Olney, Susan Faxon; Dryfhout, John, et al. *A Circle of Friends: Art Colonies of Cornish and Dublin.* Durham, N.H.: University Art Galleries, 1985.

Platt, Charles. *Italian Gardens.* New York: Harper and Brothers, 1894 (reprinted by Sagapress, Inc., 1993).

Pressley, Marion and Cynthia Zaitzevsky. *Cultural Landscape Report for Saint-Gaudens National Historic Site.* Boston: National Park Service, 1993.

Saint-Gaudens, Homer, ed. *The Reminiscences of Augustus Saint-Gaudens.* New York: Century, 1913.

Shelton, Louise. *Beautiful Gardens in America.* New York: Charles Scribner's Sons, 1915.

Shurcliff, Margaret. Lively Days: *Some Memories of Margaret Homer Shurcliff.* Taipei: Literature House, 1965.

Tankard, Judith B. *The Gardens of Ellen Biddle Shipman.* New York: Harry N. Abrams/Sagapress, inc., 1996.

Wade, Hugh Mason. *A Brief History of Cornish, 1763-1974.* Hanover, N.H.: University Press of New England, 1976.

Walker, Laura M. *Memories.* Privately printed, 1938.

Yount, Sylvia. *Maxfield Parrish, 1870-1966.* New York: Harry N. Abrams/Pennsylvania Academy of the Fine Arts, 1999.

Zea, Philip, and Norwalk, Nancy, editors. *Choice White Pines and Good Land: A History of Plainfield and Meriden,* New Hampshire. Portsmouth, N.H.: Peter E. Randall, 1991.

Articles

Clayton, Virginia T. "Reminiscence and Revival, the Old-Fashioned Garden 1890-1910," *The Magazine Antiques,* April 1990, 892-905.

Colby, Virginia Reed. "Stephen and Maxfield Parrish in New Hampshire," *The Magazine Antiques,* June 1979, 1290-98.

Crawford, "Homes and Gardens of Cornish," *House Beautiful,* April 1906, 12-14.

Davis, Rosalie H. "Saint Gaudens's Sculpted World," *Horticulture,* May 1993, 34-7.

Dryfhout, John H. "The Gardens of Augustus Saint-Gaudens," *House and Garden,* December 1985, 144-51, 199.

Duncan, Frances. "An Artist's New Hampshire Garden," *Country Life in America,* March 1907, 516-20, 554-58.

Duncan, Frances. "A Cornish Garden," *Country Life in America,* March 1908, 507-8.

Duncan, Frances. "The Gardens of Cornish," *The Century Magazine,* May 1906, 3-19.

Duncan, Frances. "How To Make an Old-Fassioned Garden," *Ladies Home Journal,* April 1909, 56.

Duncan, Frances. "Maxfield Parrish's Home and How He Built It," *The Country Calendar,* September 1905, 435-37.

Earle, Alice Morse. "Old Time Flower Gardens," *Scribner's Magazine* 20 (August 1896): 161-78.

Henderson, Helen W. "An Impression of Cornish," *The Lamp,* October 1903, 185-96.

Hill, May Brawley. "Grandmother's Garden," *The Magazine Antiques,* November 1992, 726-35.

Hobbs, Susan. "Thomas Dewing in Cornish, 1885-1905," *American Art Journal* 17 (Spring 1985): 3-22.

Martin, Jennifer. "Portraits of Flowers: The Out-of-Door Still-Life Paintings of Maria Oakey Dewing," *American Art Review* 4 (December 1977): 48-55, 114-18.

Morgan, Keith N. "Charles A. Platt's Houses and Gardens in Cornish, New Hampshire," *The Magazine Antiques*, July 1982, 117-29.

Mount, May Wilkinson. "The Gardens of Cornish," *Suburban Life*, March 1914, 133-36, 184.

Nichols, Rose Standish. "A Hilltop Garden in New Hampshire," *House Beautiful*, March 1924, 237-39, 290.

Nichols, Rose Standish. "How Not to Make a Flower Garden," *House Beautiful*, September 1911, 103.

Noble, William. "Northcote: An Artist's New Hampshire Garden," *Journal of the New England Garden History Society* 2 (Fall 1992): 1-9.

Shipman, Ellen. "The Saint-Gaudens Memorial Gardens," *Bulletin of the Garden Club of America*, May 1948, 61-5.

Tankard, Judith B. "Gardens of Saint-Gaudens," *Old-House Interiors*, Spring 1997, 67-71.

Wise, Herbert C. "A Day at Northcote, New Hampshire," *House and Garden* (June 1902): 240-51.

Archives and Unpublished Material

Chesterwood, Stockbridge, Mass.: Papers of Daniel Chester French

Cornish Colony Museum, Cornish, N.H. Alma Gilbert Archives: Parrish family letters

Rare and Manuscript Collections, Cornell University Libraries, Ithaca, N.Y.: Papers of Ellen Biddle Shipman

Saint-Gaudens National Historic Site, Cornish, N.H.: information on Cornish Colony artists

Special Collections, Dartmouth College Library, Hanover, N.H.: Papers of Herbert Adams, Winston Churchill, Daniel Chester French, Frances Duncan, Frances Grimes, Lucia Fairchild Fuller, Parrish family, Saint-Gaudens family, and others

Meador, Deborah Kay. "The Making of a Landscape Architect: Ellen Biddle Shipman and Her Years at the Cornish Art Colony." M.L.A. thesis, Cornell University, 1989.

Trumbull, Margery P. "Selections from the Published Writings of Rose Standish Nichols." M.A. thesis, Dartmouth College, 1989.

Van Buren, Deborah. "The Cornish Colony: Expressions of Attachment to Place, 1895-1915." Ph.D. diss, George Washington University, 1987.

Art Work Sources

*Except as noted below, all transparencies of Maxfield Parrish art works are the personal property of Alma Gilbert.

Adams, Herbert. *Flora*. 1929. Private Collection. Courtesy of Peter S. Nyboer

Adams, Herbert. *Girl with Water Lilies*. 1928. Private Collection. Courtesy of Peter S. Nyboer

Adams, Herbert. *The Infant Burbank*. 1905. Private Collection. Courtesy Peter S. Nyboer

Churchill, Winston. *Mrs. Spaulding's House*. Circa 1913. Peter and Alma Smith Collection

Dewing, Maria Oakey. *The Garden in May*. 1895. National Museum of American Art, Smithsonian Institution, Washington, D.C. Gift of John Gellatly.

Dewing, Maria Oakey. *Irises and Calla Lilies*. Circa 1890-1905. Detroit Institute of Arts. Founders Society Purchase, Dexter M. Ferry Jr. Fund

Dewing, Thomas Wilmer. *The Song*. 1891. Private Collection. Courtesy of Edward and Deborah Shein

French, Daniel Chester. *Mary and Margaret French*. 1893. Collection of Chesterwood, Stockbridge, Mass

French, Daniel Chester. *Victory: Model for the First Division Memorial*. 1921-24. Peter and Alma Smith Collection

Grimes, Frances. *Portrait of Anne Parrish*. 1905. U.S. Department of the Interior, Saint-Gaudens National Historic Site. Gift of the Maxfield Parrish Museum, Plainfield, N.H. Courtesy of Alma Gilbert

Hart, William Howard. *Portrait of Mrs. Herbert Adams*. 1899. George Reed and Yvonne Mathieu Collection

Hyde, William Henry. *Landscape in Cornish*. Circa 1908. Peter and Alma Smith Collection

Metcalf, Willard. *In the Garden*. 1878. Peter and Alma Smith Collection. Courtesy of Spanierman Gallery, New York

Metcalf, Willard. *Winter Afternoon*. 1917. Private Collection. Photo courtesy Berry-Hill Galleries, New York

Parrish, Maxfield. *Agib in the Enchanted Palace*. 1905. Detroit Institute of Arts. Bequest of the Estate of Dollie May Fisher

Parrish, Maxfield. *Daybreak*. 1923. Private Collection

Parrish, Maxfield. *Janion's Maple*. 1956. Private Collection

Parrish Maxfield. *Land of Make-Believe*. 1905. Private Collection

Parrish, Maxfield. *Poet's Dream*. 1901. Private Collection

Parrish, Maxfield. *Moonlight Night, Winter*. 1942. Rare Books Department, Free Library of Philadelphia

Parrish, Maxfield. *Ottauquechee River*. 1929. Private Collection

Parrish, Maxfield. *A Shower of Fragrance*. Cover for *Ladies Home Journal*. 1912. Private Collection

Parrish, Maxfield. *Whitney Panel One (North Wall)*. 1918. Whitney Family Collection

Parrish, Maxfield and Tiffany, Louis Comfort. *Dream Garden*. 1915. Estate of John W. Merriam, Philadelphia. Photo from the archives of Alma Gilbert. Gift of John W. Merriam

Parrish, Stephen. *Fecamp*. 1880. Peter and Alma Smith Collection

Parrish, Stephen. *Garden Staircase*. Circa 1907. Private Collection

Parrish Stephen. *Northcote*. Circa 1912. Corporate Art Collection, The Reader's Digest Association Inc.

Parrish, Stephen. *Pergola at Northcote*. Circa 1905. Private Collection

Platt, Charles. *Dry Goods Store*. 1881. Peter and Alma Smith Collection

Platt, Charles. *Garden in Winter* (the Croly Garden). Circa 1904. Platt family Collection. Courtesy of members of the Platt family

Platt, Charles. *High Court*. Circa 1892. Platt family Collection. Courtesy of members of the Platt family

Platt, Charles. *Larkspur*. 1895. Platt family Collection. Courtesy of members of the Platt family

Prellwitz, Edith. *Saint-Gaudens Garden*. 1898. U. S. Department of the Interior, National Park Service. Saint-Gaudens National Historic Site, Cornish, N.H.

Remington, Frederic. *Coming Through the Rye*. 1902. Peter and Alma Smith Collection

Saint-Gaudens, Augustus. *Cornish Celebration Presentation Plaque*. 1905. Peter and Alma Smith Collection

Vonnoh, Robert. *Mrs. Woodrow Wilson and Her Three Daughters*. 1913. Woodrow Wilson House, Washington, D.C.

Walker, Henry O. *The Gift Bearer*. 1892. Winner of medal at the World's Columbian Exposition, Chicago. Private Collection

Wilson, Ellen Axson. *The Terrace*. 1913. Private Collection. Courtesy of the Woodrow Wilson House, Washington, D.C.

Photo Credits

*Unless otherwise noted, all new copy photography is by Fred English and all color photography is the work of David Putnam and these photos are the personal property of Alma Gilbert.

Berry-Hill Galleries: 103
Grace Bulkeley: 5, 121
Chesterwood: 9
Cornell University Library: 50, 62
Cornish Historical Society: 67
Thomas Crane: 34 (lower)
Dartmouth College Library: 3, 4, 6, 8, 12, 14, 15, 17, 18, 19, 20, 21, 24, 25, 26, 29, 30, 31, 34, 39, 52, 56, 59, 61, 85, 86, 87, 114, 117, 118
Detroit Institute of Arts: 47, 54
Fred English: 31, 32 (upper right), 36 (upper),
Free Library of Philadelphia: 14
Alma Gilbert Collection: i, ii–iii, vi, 3, 137, 50, 52, 108, 111, 112, 113, 115
Hirschl and Adler Galleries: 19, 32,
John Layton: 1, 15, 28, 35 (all three), 37 (left),
Bill Noble: 84
Peter S. Nyboer: 32, 94, 95, 96, 97
Plainfield Historical Society: 41, 98 (Jeffrey Nintzel, photographer)
Platt Family: iv, 9, 53, 68, 69, 71, 72, 73, 74, 75, 77, 78
David Putnam: 26, 27, 37, 39, 55, 57, 58, 60, 63, 70, 71, 75, 76, 79, 80, 81, 83, 85, 86 (right), 87, 91, 92, 93, 109, 110, 112, 114, 120, 122, 123

The Reader's Digest Corporate Art Collection: 44
Saint-Gaudens National Historic Site: 10, 30 (Jeffrey Nintzel, photographer), 58, 67
Edward and Deborah Shein: 66
Jacqueline Walker Smith: 11
Smithsonian Institution: 7, 66
Sothebys: 22-23
Society for the Preservation of New England Antiques: 116
Spanierman Gallery: 36,
Nancy Angell Streeter: 46, 49, 51, 52, 99, 100, 101, 102
Judith B. Tankard: 40, 42–43, 45, 46, 47, 48, 60, 63, 64, 65, 67, 82, 90, 92, 101, 102, 103, 104, 105, 107, 119, 123
Margery P. Trumbull: 88, 89
John and Connie White: 13
Woodrow Wilson House: 45, 119 (left)

Index